A Manual of Primitive and Modern Leather Skills

Larry J. Wells

Third Printing, December, 1991

International Standard Book Number
0-88290-304-7

Library of Congress Card Catalog Number
85-080211

Horizon Publishers' Catalog and Order Number
1232

Printed and distributed
in the United States of America by

Horizon
Publishers
& Distributors, Incorporated
P.O. Box 490 Bountiful, Utah 84011-0490

Contents

Introduction

Before written history mankind began a beautiful relationship with leather. Animal skins provided the first clothing and were one key to man's survival. In one of the earliest written histories, the book of Genesis 3:21, it states "Unto Adam also and to his wife did the Lord God make coats of skins, and clothed them." Although the golden age of leather—the buffalo culture—has become a forgotten history, leather has survived and prospered.

Unlike synthetics, leather has durability, workability, and beauty that enhances with age. For this reason it has survived the Industrial Age and is making a grandstand play in the age of synthetics.

Leather is a medium for the survivalist, mountain man, cowboy, farmer, city dweller, and true craftsman. With leather you can make beautiful and useful items for yourself. This book will show you how to do it—easily.

Leather Makin' will tell you step by step how to buy and work with leather; what kind, size or weight of leather to use for what you want to create; how to cut, punch, and stitch, and how to use primitive methods with handmade tools. The latest and greatest modern approaches are also included.

The information is presented in a manner the novice will find easy to follow. Once the skills are learned the most advanced product can be self-designed and made using these basics.

Get to know your local leather dealer—ask questions. Working with leather is fun, easy, and beautiful. Let's Go!

Chapter 1

Leather Basics

Nothing brings a need for body deodorant faster than sauntering into the local leather store to buy a "little leather" for your first project. You are faced with what appears to be hundreds of rolls of leather in a multitude of colors, thicknesses, and varying degrees of softness. Then the salesman starts talking about oil tan, vegetable tan, chrome tan, deerskin, cow, pig, sheep hides, sides, splits, and skivers.

Armpits tingle, palms moisten, and the impulse to disappear sweeps you out the nearest door—without the "little leather" you came for.

What was he talking about? What did the strange words mean?

Leather Terms

Hide: A full-size skin of a large animal such as domestic cattle or horse.

Kip: The skin of a large calf or small steer generally softer than the hide of an adult animal. With modern tanning methods almost any hide can be made thin and soft, but a kip is a younger, thinner skin.

Side: Half of any animal skin, generally a large animal such as a domestic cow. It is cut full length down the spine of the animal so the side includes the head, shoulder, front leg, back, and back leg.

Skiver: A very thin top-grain layer split from a sheepskin. They are extremely soft and pliable but lack strength. They work well for a lining or backing, providing a soft finish to stronger leather.

Skin: The term generally referring to a small animal's hide with the hair left on in the tanning process; rabbit skin,

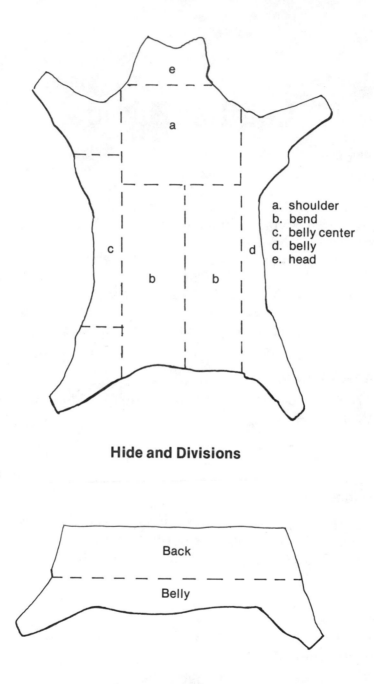

a. shoulder
b. bend
c. belly center
d. belly
e. head

Hide and Divisions

Half Side and Divisions

sheepskin, etc. It may, however, be the hide of a small animal without the hair left on.

Leather Splits

Most commercially tanned hides are split into as many as four layers. Thin hides like a kip give fewer layers. Sole leather is not split at all.

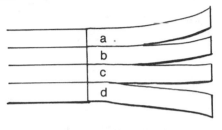

a. top or full grain   c. split
b. deep buff or split   d. slab or split

Splits of Leather

Top Grain: This is the cut from the hair-side of an animal's skin. Top grain is sometimes buffed and treated, or smoothed. It can be the strongest and most durable leather when taken from cattle, horse, or pig. Top grain of smaller animals provides an excellent garment leather. It is sold by the square foot.

Full Grain: This is also the cut from the hair-side of the skin, but has not been buffed, reduced, or smoothed. It is sold by the square foot.

Split: Any layer from under the top grain may be called a "split." Leathers advertised as splits are from the under layers. Splits are not as strong as top grain, but they may be finished off smooth to appear as top grain, or finished as suede. Splits are sold by the square foot.

Slab: Technically, the bottom cut or the cut from the flesh-side of the animal's skin is called a "slab" although often all inter-cuts are called splits. Slab is often made into a very soft, fine suede to be used for garments. It is sold by the square foot.

Types of Leather

Vegetable Tan: Uses tree bark combined with chemicals. In the past, vegetable tanning required weeks. Now chemicals speed the process to days. Oak and vegetable tans are the same. Only vegetable-tan leathers will shape and stay to form when wet (as will be explained in chapter 4). Vegetable-tan leather will not take repeated heavy oilings, nor can it be washed. The oil causes the core of the leather to rot so that the leather may go stiff after washing. Vegetable tan is used for tooling leather and can be used for gun scabbards since it will not affect the bluing on the gun.

Chrome Tan: Accomplished in a few hours, chrome tan produces a blue-green colored leather that is generally dyed. The leather can be washed and it works well for garments, moccasins, or any item that will be exposed to dirt and weather. It stays flexible after repeated wettings and has good long-wearing abilities. Chrome tan will not withstand repeated heavy oilings because the core will rot. Chrome-tan leather can be found by cutting the leather and checking for the blue-green center, or by placing the leather in boiling, or warm, water. Fold the wet, boiled leather. Chrome tan will spring back to its original form while vegetable tan will fold and stay like paper.

Chrome tan may also be processed in an additional vegetable tan to give the leather some of those qualities.

Oil Tan: Preserves the hide by saturating the fibers with oil and waxes. It is a tough, long-wearing leather that can be heavily oiled to restore the softness when it has been subjected to extreme moisture conditions. Oil tan is a heavy leather because of the quantity of oil in it. This leather will not breathe well and it is uncomfortable for shirts, dresses, etc., but it works well for chaps and any article that will receive severe wear or moisture. It comes in varying degrees of oil and wax ratios.

Latigo Leather: A top-grain cut. Latigo should be used whenever the finished product will be subject to weather and heavy wear. It works well for mukluk and moccasin soles. Sold by the square foot.

Chamois: A split from sheepskin. When chrome tanned it is good for garments that will be subjected to water or weather. It is extremely soft, supple, and thin. It does not, however, withstand heavy wear. Sold by the square foot.

Sole Leather: A vegetable-tan leather made especially for shoe and sandal soles. It comes in a variety of thicknesses and is measured in "irons." (See below.) Sole will be stiff and thick and it is very resilient to wear. Normally sold by the pound.

Harness Backs or Harness Leather: An extremely sturdy leather made for harness and riding—or packing—tack. It is thick and stiff with a fairly heavy wax content. Harness is long-wearing and it will hold its shape even under abusive wear. Sold by the pound.

Buckskin: Originally from the male deer and tanned with a brain-tan process then smoked to get the light tan "buckskin" color. Generally, if advertised as "buckskin," it is tanned deer hide, but you should ask. Buckskin is a very supple, long-wearing leather that makes nice garments. Sold by the square foot.

Rawhide: An untreated animal hide which comes from any animal, although domestic cow is what's sold in the leather shops. Depending on the animal hide—and the way it was treated—it can be rock-hard or slightly pliable. Used where an indestructible surface is needed, or where it can be applied wet and shrunk to size—or shape—as it dries. Generally sold by the "bend" (see below) or side.

Weights and Sizes of Leather

Bend: A variable measure of hide. A rawhide bend is about one foot by two feet while a sole leather bend is about two and one-half feet by three feet. A bend comes from the back of the animal. It is the thickest leather.

Iron: The thickness of sole leather. One iron is 1/48 of an inch thick.

Ounces: Leather thickness is described in ounces. One ounce is equal to 1/64 of an inch-thick leather. (All measures of leather are "give or take a little." This is why a piece will be listed as "2-3 oz." or "6-7 oz."—and even two pieces marked "3-4 oz." will feel different in their thickness.) Hides will run from 2 to 10 ounces in thickness. Although they are referred to by ounces they will be sold by the square foot.

Square Foot: The measure by which most leather is sold. On the flesh-side of the hide there is a large number with a small number—1, 2, or 3—beside it. The large number is square feet, the small number the fraction of a square foot. One equals ¼ square foot, 2 equals ½ square foot, and 3 equals ¾ square foot. This measurement is done at the tannery before shipping.

Measuring Leather for Patterns

It a pattern calls for 36-inch wide material, multiply the yards required by nine (nine square feet per square yard). To compensate for the cutting loss, add 15 percent of the total. For example, if two yards are called for calculate the following:

2 yds. × 9 = 18 sq. ft.
15% × 18 sq. ft. = 2¾ sq. ft.
18 sq. ft. + 2¾ sq. ft. = 20¾ sq. ft.
20¾ sq. ft. of leather needed.

If possible, lay the pattern out on the leather piece before you buy it. Leather comes in odd shapes and has sections of unusable pieces so that what appears to be enough may not be. By placing the pattern you plan to use on different shapes you may decrease the amount of waste and thus save money.

By buying in bulk you can often receive a discount. The more hides purchased, up to a breaking point, the more discount available. Some leather outlets will negotiate the marked price. It's worth a try.

Chapter 2

Making Leather

Folks who live where they can obtain their own fresh hides should give tanning a whirl. It's not complicated and you really don't have to talk yourself—or your mate—into chewing on the smelly old thing. Tanning saves money and imparts a mighty good feeling when you are wearing something you shot, skinned, tanned, and made totally by using your own ingenuity.

Under home tanning methods, animal skins will differ. Some will produce more and some less desirable easy-to-tan leathers. Trying to tan the wrong skin (especially on your first tanning adventure) can result in a lot of stomping, huffing, puffing, and colorful adjectives. These outbursts will put pressure on the family relationship which is already strained because of the containers of smelly "solution" and "rotten" hides that have been sitting around the house to maintain their temperature. All you have to do is add hair and bits of raw fat to plug the kitchen sink after you wash that "stinking" badger skin and your "mountain-man days" in the same lodge may become limited.

Let's start with the right animal skin.

Hides and Their Tannability

Following is a list of animals and ease of tannability of their hides starting with the easiest and moving down to the hides that are harder to tan:

antelope
deer
elk   } all about equal
domestic sheep
domestic rabbit
moose

muskrat
mustelidae family
dog family
beaver
bear
domestic cattle

For a first tanning project domestic rabbit is good. It tans easily when fresh and—because of its size—can be handled and worked without trouble.

White rabbit provides the most durable hide with durability becoming less the darker the hair. Black is thinnest and weakest. Wild rabbit hides are very thin and easily ripped which makes them extremely hard to work with although they will tan softly. (They can also be used without tanning. See chapter 5.)

Young animal hides make the most pliable leather with female hides softer than male hides. Males have the strongest, thickest leather. And the fresher the hide, the better the end product will be with the least effort.

Skinning

Hanging by the Head

The quality of a leather piece begins with the skinning of the animal. The animals listed as easy to tan are also easy to skin. Skinning should be done without a knife as much as possible. The less flesh and fat left on a hide at the time of skinning, the less work on the fleshing. The fewer nicks and cuts in the skin the more usable the leather will be when it's completed.

An animal's skin removes with the least effort and with the least remaining flesh and fat when removal is started at the head. Hang the animal by its head with a strong rope. The pelt is slit up the belly from the genitals to the cord around the neck at the base of the head. All four legs are split from the slit going up the belly to the knee and around the knee joint. Cut around the genitals, anal opening, and the milk bag (if there is one). The tail can be cut off with the anus.

Begin skinning at the neck. The neck on most animals is hard to skin because the hide fits tight and must be removed

Cut hide on dashed line.
Peel off from neck down.

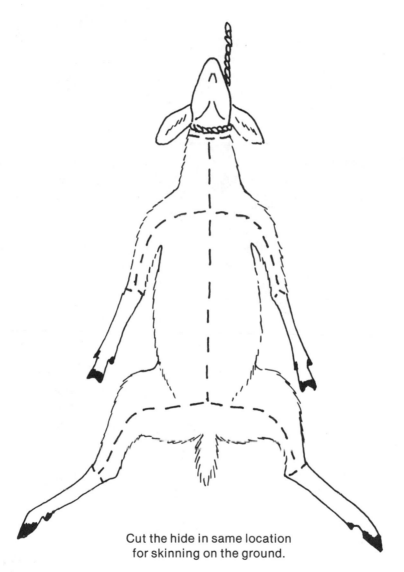

Cut the hide in same location
for skinning on the ground.

Hanging and Skinning

with a knife. Use light cutting strokes with the tip of the blade run between the skin and the flesh while the pelt is pulled downward and outward from the neck. When the shoulders are reached, the skin can be pulled down at the same time you are using your fist to push the hide outward from the carcass. This method will remove the skin without knife marks if it is used on those animals listed as easy to tan. When an area becomes difficult, use the knife then go back to the fist.

Just below the shoulders the thin layer of flesh which lays over the ribs often starts to adhere to the hide. Use a knife blade to get it started back on the body, then continue with the fist. Work the skin down off the carcass by using pulling and pushing motions with the fist. If the hide is only pulled from the body, flesh and fat will stay with the skin which will make a lot of work when fleshing time arrives.

A 3-inch-wide wedge-shaped limb or board can be used if the fist gets sore from pushing. Rubber gloves will generally prevent the problem of sore hands.

Or an air pressure hose can be used to remove the hide. Insert the nozzle into the area between the skin and the carcass and hold the hide down to seal air loss. By working with this process the hide can be "blown" off the flesh, then slit and removed. This leaves a clean skin.

Skinning Large Animals

Large animals such as elk and moose must be skinned on the ground unless they are quartered which will destroy the size of the finished leather piece. Begin by turning the animal parallel with the slope—head uphill if possible.

I shot my first elk in country standing at the same angle as a domestic cow's face—almost straight up and down. To add to the challenge, it was just at dark when the bull walked in front of my sights and I was standing deep in central Idaho wilderness.

My 145 pounds trying to roll 600 pounds up and down the hill and onto its back was just that—a try, half-hearted. I propped the elk the best I could and opened the stomach cavity while I was kneeling below the carcass.

The bull was laying slightly on his side with the underside facing downhill. When the belly was opened "Wapiti" decided to roll down the hill and sit on my lap. Trying to get away and from under the romantic critter was like an ant in an ant-lion trap. The more I wiggled the more the heavy quarter-ton settled on my thighs, pinning my doubled-up legs to the ground.

A vision of my body spending the night—maybe several nights— squished under the bloody, foul-smelling carcass of the male elk flashed in the darkness which now engulfed me. That vision flittered into the blackness to be quickly replaced with the sounds of bears, lions, cougars, wolves, tigers, vampires—maybe even coyotes—coming to the smell of blood. Fear, that great motivator of genius, jammed my brain in gear and brought a repulsive—but possible— solution for my survival.

The bull was not cooperating with my feeble efforts to move it, but gravity was and it kept moving the elk down, more on top of me. I could roll the animal downhill, although downhill meant over the top of my body. And that meant the open stomach cavity also had to roll over the top of my body. Like a limbo dancer I lay back with my head down the slope.

My bloody, elk-smelling body crawled out on the uphill side of the dead bull, free at last.

Turn that animal parallel to the hill!

Rocks and small logs can be used to prop the body on its back. Slit the skin as described under "hanging by the head." Start skinning at the chest and work the skin back with the fist as much as possible. (Spare the knife!) When halfway down one side, remove the blocks from the opposite side and turn the body on that side. Continue skinning the up side until you are over the backbone. Spread the hide out—keeping the flesh-side clean—and roll the carcass over on the skin to keep the meat clean. Skin the up side in the same manner until joining the other skinned area near the backbone.

The animal can then be quartered—or boned out—and removed from the skin.

Skinning Small Animals

Small animals, like rabbits, are easier to work with if they are hung from their back legs although they will skin cleaner if they are skinned from the head down. If several rabbits are to

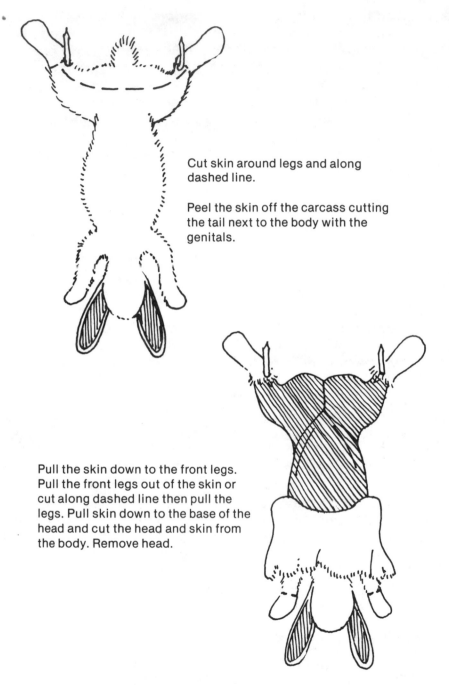

Cut skin around legs and along dashed line.

Peel the skin off the carcass cutting the tail next to the body with the genitals.

Pull the skin down to the front legs. Pull the front legs out of the skin or cut along dashed line then pull the legs. Pull skin down to the base of the head and cut the head and skin from the body. Remove head.

Skinning Small Animals

be skinned, drive two 16-penny nails shoulder high in a post or tree. (Cut the nail heads off after they are driven in.) The nails are placed between the Achilles tendons and the leg bone on the back legs with the underside facing you. Cut the skin around the back legs at the "knee joint," slit across and past the genitals, up the other leg, and around the joint. Work the skin from the legs with your fingers. (The tail is cut off with the genitals.) Then pull the skin down over the body to the front legs. The front legs can be pulled from the skin and the covering worked down to the base of the head where it is cut off.

If any skin is to be tanned later, it should be salted after the fleshing process. The hide is laid out flesh-side up and non-iodized salt spread and rubbed into it. The skin is then folded flesh-side together and rolled up. It should be placed on a slant—where it can drain fluids—and left for three days. Lay it out again, hair-side down, and resalt, then lay out to dry. The hide should keep for six months with no problem.

After fleshing, the skin can be rolled up—hair-side out—and placed in the deep-freeze. It will keep about six months without freezer burn if the flesh-side is not exposed.

Remember, however, that a fresh skin is the easiest to tan, a frozen second best, and a salted hide last.

Tanning Tools and Hide Preparation

Tanning tools are a personal preference item; what works for one person will not necessarily work as well for another. There are some general categories of tools. They may be purchased (see listing in chapter 6) or made from what is lying around the yard or house. Stainless steel is preferred but not necessary.

Primitive Tools

Primitive tools are made from materials at hand. The wider your knowledge of primitive skills the greater your ability to use what is available for your needs. Materials I will mention may not be found where you live but with experimentation and a concept of what you need in tools, you can create them from natural materials in the same way early man did—without a hardware store.

Stakes—Fleshing Beams

Fleshing is the first step in any tanning process. Under primitive conditions the hide is generally staked out on the ground, flesh-side up. This requires enough stakes (preferably hardwood) to be placed every 6 to 12 inches around the skin. For a bull elk the stakes should be 12 inches long and at least ¾-inch in diameter. Remember that there will be a lot of pressure on these stakes later when you stake the hide to dry.

If a down, barkless log at least 18 inches in diameter is handy, the skin can be tossed over that for scraping. The hide is fastened to the log by making several ¼- to ¾-inch diameter, 2-inch-long pegs. The sticks (again hardwood is preferred) are wedge-shaped on one end and blunt on the other. With a knife blade a slit is made in the hide and in the log by pushing the blade into the hide and on through to the log. The blade should be placed parallel to the grain of the log. The wedge-end of the pins are placed in the slits and driven into the log through the skin. They will hold better if the hide is placed over the end of the log (seldom possible in nature) and the pegs placed in the end.

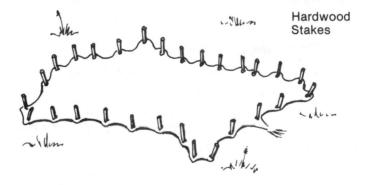

Hardwood Stakes

Primitive Scraping

In "modern" primitive camps, a pole "stretching frame" is often used. It is made by planting two posts in the ground two feet wider than the largest hide it will be used for. A pole is lashed to the top and the bottom, again leaving an area at least two feet wider than the largest hide to be stretched will be. Holes are punched in the skin with a bone awl, then cordage is threaded through the holes. The hide is then tied and stretched to the frame. Now the skin can be scraped.

It is not likely under truly primitive conditions that enough cordage would be available for this method as nomadic wanderers (as was primitive man) seldom created anything that was this time-consuming and permanent.

Scrapers

All that is required of a scraper is that it have an edge that—when pushed or pulled over the flesh-side of the hide—will remove flesh, fat, and other unwanted tissue. A chip of stone works well. On skins draped over a log, the rib bone of a large animal (deer or larger) will do the job. If teeth are carved into the narrow edge of the bone by filing with the chip of a rock it improves the effectiveness. A femur bone of a large animal can be cut near the knee-joint end at a 60-degree angle and teeth filed in the protruding edge to make an effective flesh remover. A chip of stone—or piece of iron—can be mounted on the trimmed eye-guard of an elk antler leaving some of the beam for a handle. This forms an adze-shaped tool that is easy to use on a hide staked to the ground.

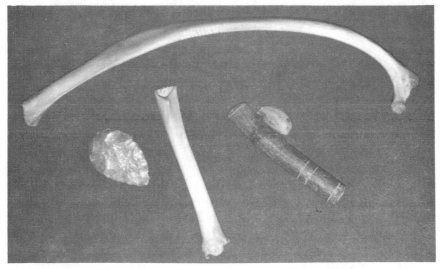

Primitive Scrapers
Top: rib bone. Bottom (left to right): stone blade; deer femur bone; stone blade mounted in wood handle.

Drying—Stretching

The same wooden stakes used to stake the skin for flesh-ing are used to stake the cleaned hide to the ground for drying and stretching. It is during this use that the importance of stakes in proper sizes is apparent: a tremendous pressure is placed on the pins as the hide dries and tries to shrink so that if the stakes are not long enough to be driven deep into the ground they will pull out. And if they are not large enough in diameter they will break.

The "stretching frame" (described in primitive fleshing beams) can be used for this stage. Again, the cordage that ties the skin to the frame must be strong.

Softening or Staking Tools

The skin must be worked over a dull edge—like shining shoes—to soften and become "tanned." In nature, this dull edge can be the broken end of a stump, a rib bone anchored between two trees, or a rope stretched between two trees. Sometimes a rope loop is used to pull the hide through using a back and forth motion.

The stretching frame is also used for softening. The hide is tied in place, as stated, then—using a bone or dull-edged tool—the hide is softened by "scraping" the tanned skin with the tool.

Awl

Any tool that will poke a hole in the hide or leather will work as an awl. Early man used bone and antlers until metal was available, then he changed to iron.

The bone awl is generally made from the foreleg of a deer or a sheep. The bone is split by "sawing" with a stone chip along the natural groove which runs the full length of the bone on both sides. When the groove is worn deep enough the bone is split by pounding. The split half is then cut in half and ground to a point by working on a sand stone or by shaving down with a chip of stone or glass. The natural, rounded joint is left on top for a handle.

Antler tine can be ground to a point in the same manner but care must be taken not to go into the porous core.

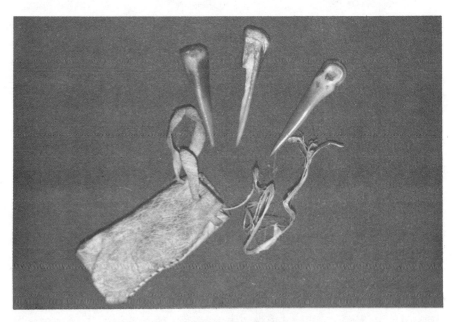

Primitive Awls
Top (left to right): blunt bone awl, used to push sinew through holes; sharp bone awls made from foreleg of a deer. Bottom: deerskin awl carry case with sinew "thread."

Awls can also be made from hardwood such as mountain mahogany, scrub oak, serviceberry, or chokecherry. The wood should be cut green and allowed to dry slowly in the shade for at least a month. After the curing time, the wood is fashioned into the desired shape.

Modern Tools

Modern tanning tools can be purchased and they are designed for a specific job, but many articles around the home can be modified to do the same job as the "store-bought" tools. Stainless steel is preferred but, if the tool is cleaned up after every use, any metal will work.

As stated in primitive tanning tools, the ability to adapt what you have to what you need can provide good, practical, "modern" tanning tools.

Containers

A 10-gallon or larger non-metallic container is needed for dehairing and chemical tanning solutions. A 30-gallon is more convenient for dehairing. A plastic garbage can works without much expense but a ceramic crock, a wooden barrel, or a heavy-duty plastic barrel is more durable. The container should have a lid.

A wooden paddle—or stirring stick—long enough to reach the bottom and strong enough to lift heavy, wet hides will also be needed.

Fleshing Beam

A fleshing beam is made from a log 18 to 24 inches in diameter, 6 feet long and split lengthwise so the resulting slab is at least 6 inches thick. The surface is smoothed with a draw knife, or plane, so that there are no protrusions to tear or poke holes in the skin lying on it. A stand is made to raise one end about chest high. This stand is fastened to the slab, leaving about 12 inches of the slab as an overhang. The bottom end of the beam is placed on a stand 12 inches off the ground. Hooks or spikes can be embedded in the top end on the underside as a place to attach the hide. This will hold it in place while scraping is done.

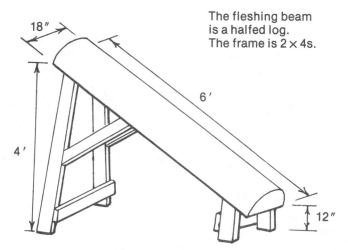

18″

The fleshing beam is a halfed log. The frame is 2 × 4s.

6′

4′

12″

Fleshing Beam

If the above materials are not available, an 18-inch-diameter, 6-foot-long log can be leaned up against the fence, wall, or whatever, and nails can be driven through the hide into the upper end of the log. The log must still be smoothed so that no holes will be pushed through the skin when the scraper passes over one of the protrusions.

Scrapers

The most effective commercial scrapers are built similar to a draw knife. They have teeth on one side of the blade and a smooth blade on the other.

I have found many items that can be used as a scraper but an edge with teeth is the most effective. A large stainless steel serving spoon with teeth filed around the edge works well. The handle must be reinforced or it might bend and eventually break. An old draw-blade with teeth filed on one side works as will some fish scrapers. Any piece of metal that can have handles attached on both ends and teeth filed on one edge will do the job. The teeth should not be too sharp or they will cut the skin; just use a serrated edge to allow the fat and flesh to catch.

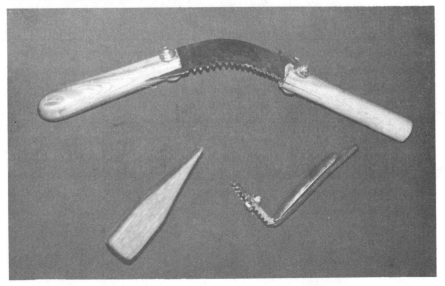

Modern Scrapers and Slicker
Top: two-handled "draw" scraper. Bottom (left to right): hardwood slicker; single-handle scraper made from "fish scaler."

Two types of scraper are generally needed; one like a draw knife to pull with both hands, taking off most of the unwanted tissue. The second type is one used with one hand that is able to get at small, inconvenient spots that a big blade does not reach.

Slicker

A slicker is made of hardwood to squeegee excess water and chemicals out of the hide. It should be 3 to 5 inches wide, one inch thick and 4 to 6 inches long. It is wedge-shaped on one end.

Softening Stake

Softening stakes are best if they're made from hardwood, but I have used one made from Douglas fir for 15 years and it still works well. It is made from a 2-inch-by-6-inch-by-3-foot board. One end is fastened to a base stand so it will stand up and allow you to use your feet to hold it solid while the hide is worked. The upper end is wedge-shaped, forming a dull edge to work the skin over.

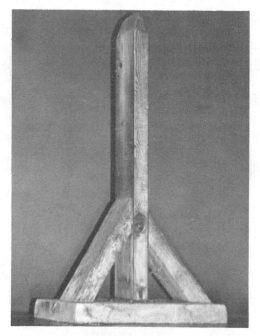

Softening Stake

Drying Frame

The drying frame is made from 2 by 4s to form a square, or rectangle. The frame should be two feet larger in all directions than the largest hide to be tanned. Corner-bracing is suggested because a drying hide puts a lot of pressure on the frame. A willow hoop can be made for small skins such as rabbitskins. The hides are attached to the frames by a wire hook which can be purchased, or made from any heavy wire such as a heavy clothes hanger. The wire hook is poked through the edge of the skin and attached to heavy string such as a parachute cord. The cord is then tied securely to the frame.

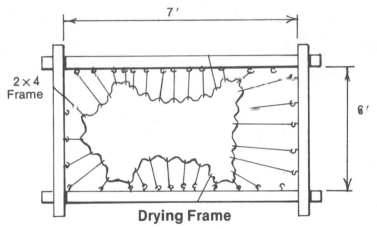

Drying Frame

Modern Awl

An awl is a metal spike used to poke holes in the skin. It can be made from a nail, a broken screwdriver, or any item that can be ground—or filed—to a sharp, tapering point. They are available, commercially, at leather outlet stores.

Sometimes an awl is needed to make holes for hooks used to stretch the hide.

Tanning Process

Primitive Tanning

There are several ways to tan a skin using primitive tanning agents such as the brains and spinal cords, or a mixture of brains, spinal cords, and liver, but the principal tanning

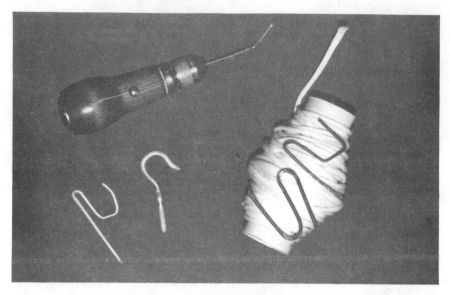

Hooks and Awl
Top: stitching awl. Bottom (left to right): curtain hook used to attach cord to hide; screw hook used to attach cord to drying frame; parachute cord to stretch hide to drying frame; two homemade wire hooks made from coat hangers setting on the cord.

agent is the oil. (Brains have a high tallow content). Homemade soap or animal fat can be used as a substitute for brains in the primitive process. Animal fat tends to go rancid on the leather which causes a strong odor whereas brains do not, but the finished product is the same.

Fleshing the Hide

The hide is staked out on the ground or lain over a down log flesh-side up as described above. Using a scraper, all flesh and fat is removed from the skin. A rib-bone scraper on the log or a leg-bone scraper on the ground will remove the large areas and clean most of the skin. A small stone scraper, or leg-bone scraper, will hit the tough spots to finish it up. The finished product should appear white—or blue-white—with no membrane, flesh, or fat adhering to the skin.

If the skin is exceptionally fat, urine will help cut the greasy tissue. The hide is laid out on the ground flesh-side up and family or camp members can urinate on it. The uric acid should be left on the skin for twenty-four hours. It is then washed off and the scraping resumed.

Removing the Hair

If leather without the hair is desired the hide is first soaked in a running stream until the hair will slip. The skin must be weighted down with rocks and placed in water where dogs cannot get to it. (Dogs love to drag the smelly old things a-round.) If you are in a populated area the hides should be put where people don't go because the skins tend to disappear.

The hide is ready when the hair slips easily off by just rubbing your hand over the hide. The hair will "pull" off before it reaches the slip stage. It must reach the slip stage where it can be "pushed" off with your hand. To make buckskin, the top layer of skin—or epidermis—must also be scraped off.

If there is no running stream available, a container may be used to soak the hide but the water must be changed every day. (Even then, in warm weather the raw skin may get mighty smelly! Do not put a cover over the container or it gets worse.) A rock weight will be needed to hold all of the hide under the water. Adding wood ashes to the container of water will help speed up the dehairing process because of the lye in the ashes.

My first tanning attempt was an old buck deer in full winter coat. Not having a container I did a whole lot of story telling and got the consent of my wife for one week's use of the family bathtub. My big plan was based on what I had read which said the hair would fall off in a week of soaking, at the longest. Somehow the information (a government pamphlet) forgot to mention changing the water, or that in the warm temperature of our bathroom the hide would smell even in running water.

After three days my wife reneged on our deal. She said the neighbors were complaining that we were running an animal products factory in a residential zone, and the children were refusing to go to the bathroom, sneaking outside instead. The dead "thing" had to go!

Then came the chore of getting a very odoriferous, soaking wet, hundred-pound, magnetic hair-shedding deerskin from the bathroom, down the hall, through the living room and out the door without dripping any stench or dropping the sticky hair anywhere—period! All this was under threat of my total exile if I blew it. Only a walk to the gas chamber might compare.

It will take from one to two weeks for the hair to slip depending on how fresh the skin is and the warmth of the water. In warm water, such as in irrigation ditches, there will sometimes be a problem with aquatic insects eating holes in the skin, or rot setting in on some of the thinner areas such as under the armpits: and the skin will smell dead!

When the hair has begun to slip, remove the hide and put it on the fleshing beam, log, ground, or whatever you have. Using a draw knife or similar tool, slide the hair from the skin. A rib bone or stick will work if the hair is slipping like it should. To make buckskin, a rib bone or a draw knife is required to scrape the outer layer of skin from the hide.

The hide must be kept wet during this process. Using handfuls of the wet hair, the skin can be sponged with water

Dehairing the Hide
A log can be used at the river the skin was soaked in as a fleshing beam to remove the hair.

When the hair is removed and the epidermis scraped free, the skin is ready for the brains.

Tanning with the Hair On

All skins can be tanned with the hair on although large hides—like a cow with long hair or a sheep with long wool—tend to be very heavy when wet, and hard to handle. Deer, elk, and antelope do not have real hair; they have a hollow tube that can be tanned on, but which will break and wear off easily. Antelope hair will often pull out without soaking and will shed after tanning.

As with all skins to be tanned, the fresher the better, and tanning with the hair on is no different. The hide is first fleshed and washed then placed in the brain-tanning solution which eliminates the dehairing process.

Brain Tanning

Tho brain of the animal (if you have it) will work just fine for tanning although—depending on the size of the hide in relation to the brain—you may need more than one. Beef brains are the easiest to obtain on a commercial basis: they can be found at a local slaughter house. The brains are boiled and made into a slurry in the liquid they were boiled in. There must be enough brain solution—about hotcake-batter consistency—to cover the hide.

Preserving the Brains

The brain from a fresh kill may be boiled and then dried to be reconstituted later for tanning after the dehairing and epidermis-removal process.

The wet hide is wrung out and placed in the brain solution overnight. This solution may contain spinal cords with the brain and also boiled, mashed liver. The brains and liver should all be mashed and beaten, or run through a sieve to form an even consistency of slurry. My best results have been using the brain alone.

Working the Hide

After soaking about twenty-four hours, the hide is removed from the solution—or what is left of it as it soaks into the hide—and wrung out. The wet hide is worked as it drys over the staking tool—like shining shoes—or placed on a drying frame and worked with a bone tool. Every inch of the hide must be worked while it is drying until the hide is completely dry. This means working the skin every 15 to 30 minutes during the drying time. It is better to hang the hide in the shade so it will dry slowly while it is being worked. If an area does not soften by the time it is dry it must be redampened and reworked. If animal fat is available it may be rendered out and added to warm water to form an oil of which a thin layer can be applied to the wet hide before working. This is especially helpful if there are areas where the hide did not soften. Those areas can be redampened, oiled, and reworked with better results.

Softening the Tanned Skin
The hide with or without hair is worked back and forth as if "shining shoes" over the softening stake as skin dries to create soft leather.

Soap and Animal-Fat Tanning

Homemade lye soap which is almost 100 percent fat can be used to create a buckskin-like product. The hide is treated the same way for the dehairing and epidermis removal. If the hide is to be tanned with the hair on, it is processed the same as it is using the brains.

The soap is shaved from the bar into boiling water and dissolved. A very soapy solution is desired. After the water is cooled the wet hide is wrung out and placed in the solution, then left overnight.

The skin is removed from the solution and treated the same as the brain tan skin for softening.

In the fall, animal fat is rendered from animals that hibernate: i.e., bears, skunks, and badgers. (Rendering is the heating of fat at a low temperature but hot enough to remove the pure oil—or grease—in liquid form.) The liquid or "shortening"—if it has cooled off—is put in a warm-water solution. The water should be warm enough to keep the shortening liquid, but not any hotter than is necessary. The grease will float on top of the water. The wrung-out, dehaired hide is dunked six times in the "solution." The grease floating on top will put an even coat on the skin as it is raised out of the water on both sides. The skin is then rolled up and left in a warm place overnight.

This method does not work on hides with the hair on. To "fat tan" a hide with the hair on, use the procedure outlined below.

If no water is available rub the rendered fat on both sides of the wrung-out, dehaired skin as even as possible then roll it up and set it in a warm place overnight. If tanning is done with the hair on oil only the flesh side of the skin, being careful not to get the grease on the hair. Fold the hide over, flesh against flesh, and put it in a warm place overnight.

The fat-tanned skin is softened with the same process as the brain-tanned skin.

Smoking the Hide

A tripod frame is built of willows or other poles large enough to accommodate the number of hides to be smoked.

The hides are tied to the tripod creating a "tipi" effect. A small fire is built under the tipi and smothered with green willow or any wood that does not have heavy pitch—pine, fir, or spruce should not be used. Keep the fire small and watch carefully so you don't burn the skins. Four to six hours will give the rich "tan" color and help to keep the hide soft whether it is wet or dry.

All primitive tans must be reworked when they get wet or they will become stiff when they are dry.

Smoking the Leather
A small fire is built in the center of the "hide tipi" and fed with green willow or quaking aspen to smoke the tanned skins to the desired color.

Modern Tanning

It is much easier using modern home-tanning methods to obtain a good quality finished product than it was with the "old ways."

There are four tanning methods for today's home tanner:

Chrome tanning is used most by commercial tanneries because it delivers the best product. Chrome tan products can be washed and still retain their softness and pliability. The chemical used is chromium sulfate, thus the term "chrome tan."

Acid tanning, sometimes called "tawing," does not produce a lasting tan. The product will become stiff with repeated wetting. It is done with sulfuric acid, oxalic acid, or strong vinegar (acetic acid).

Alum tanning produces a white leather much like brain tan but, again, it is not a lasting tan. It is done with aluminum sulfate, ammonium alum, or potash alum.

Vegetable tanning takes longer and it is harder to achieve a soft product, but it is a lasting tan and has special qualities that are sometimes desired such as holding a shape after it gets wet. This tan is done with oak, sumac, hemlock, or some other bark or plant with a high tannic-acid content.

Fleshing the Hide

Place the skin on the fleshing beam flesh-side up. Using a draw knife—or scraper—remove as much fat, flesh, and membrane as possible. Putting the hide in a freezer so the fat becomes brittle will help with its removal. There will be a chance to remove more later but get all you can now.

The hide can be put in a solution of one ounce of bleach to one gallon of water (about ten gallons for a deer-sized animal) to soften a dry skin and to help make the meat and fat easier to remove from the hide. If a dry, stiff hide is being softened it should be soaked for two days.

Dehairing

If a dry, salted hide is being used it must be soaked in the bleach solution to soften before dehairing. Do not bend a dry hide. Bending will weaken the leather in the area of the bend.

Mix one pint of builder's lime (sometimes called "hydrated lime") at a lumber yard to one gallon of water. This must be mixed in a non-metallic container. Normally, ten gallons will cover a deer hide.

The skin must be thoroughly soaked before it is put into the lime solution. Put a stone on top of the hide to keep all of it under the solution. Hides of hollow-haired animals, such as deer, will float on top of the water. The hide must be turned and stirred every day. This can be done with a wooden paddle or stirring stick or it can be done by hand if rubber gloves are worn.

Depending on the temperature and freshness of the skin, it will take from one to two weeks for the hair to slip. As with the primitive dehairing, the hair must slide off just with a hand rub, not be pulled off.

When the hair has slipped remove the hide and rinse it off with a hose. Let it hang to drip for 30 minutes then put it on a fleshing beam and scrape the hair from the hide. If you are working indoors, put a sheet of visqueen or a piece of canvas on the floor under your work area. Deer and elk hair are hard to gather up since they cling to everything.

Now turn the skin over, flesh-side up, and finish removing all flesh and fat from the hide. At this point it must be completely cleaned.

Neutralizing the Hide

The lime is neutralized by one of two methods.

Method number one: Place the dehaired skin in clean water for eight hours. Change the water once during that time and "slick" the hide out with a slicker. Mix a solution of one quart of vinegar to twelve gallons of water. Soak the skin in this solution for twenty-four hours, stirring frequently. Remove the hide and slick both sides. Again, place the skin in clean water for another twenty-four hours. After removing and slicking both sides again, the skin is ready for pickling.

Method number two: Place the dehaired hide in clean water for two hours. The water should be changed and the skin slicked out several times during this time. Mix a solution of three ounces of lactic acid to eight gallons of water, or use a solution of one quart of sharp cider vinegar to three quarts of water. Eight to ten gallons will be needed to cover the skin. Soak and rinse dehaired hide in this solution for two hours. Remove the skin, slick both sides, and rinse it in clear water. Slick both sides again.

Pickling the Hide

The hide is now ready to pickle to prepare it for the tanning solution. The hide can be worked and softened, after being pickled, and used as leather. The hide will not rot, but repeated wetting will cause it to harden like a rawhide.

There are three pickling methods:

Method number one: Mix a solution of one-half ounce of concentrated sulphuric acid (which can be bought at a pharmacy) or two ounces sulphuric battery acid (available at an auto-parts house) to one pound of non-iodized salt and one gallon of water. Salt is first dissolved in water, then the acid added. Be careful! Wear goggles and rubber gloves. Do not breathe the fumes that rise when acid is added to the salt water. Stir gently as the acid is slowly added. (Caution: This solution *must* be mixed in a non-metalic container.) Place the neutralized skin in the solution. Let it soak for three days, stirring at least twice a day with a wooden stirring stick.

Method number two: Mix one ounce oxalic acid to one pound of non-iodized salt dissolved in one gallon of water. Again, be careful! (Caution: This solution *must* be in a non-metalic container.) Dissolve the salt in the water first, then slowly add the acid. Place the neutralized skin in the solution. Let it soak for three days stirring at least twice a day with a wooden stirring stick.

Method number three: Mix five gallons of white vinegar (five percent acetic acid) to ten pounds of non-iodized salt dissolved in seven gallons of water. Dissolve the salt in the water first, then add the vinegar. (Remember: This solution is to be in a non-metalic container only!) Place the neutralized skin in the solution. Let it soak for three days, stirring it at least twice a day with a wooden stirring stick.

After any of the pickling treatments remove the skin, rinse it in clear water, then slick out.

Tanning the Hide

Chrome Tanning

Mix one and one-half pounds of non-iodized salt in five gallons of water (five gallons are generally needed to cover one deerskin after it is dehaired) in a non-metalic container. Let stand.

Bring one quart of water to a boil, then mix one-half pound chromium sulfate into the boiling water. Continue boiling for five minutes. Be careful. This solution tends to stain whatever it gets on.

Put the rinsed skin into the salt solution. Let soak for 30 minutes then take the hide out of the solution. Pour half of the chromium sulfate solution into the salt water, stirring slowly. Put the skin back in the chrome and salt solution (called "tanning liquor") and leave for twelve hours, stirring the hide twice during this time. After twelve hours add the other half of the chrome solution, stirring well. Let the skin soak for five days, stirring at least twice a day.

Check to see if the tanning is complete by cutting a sliver of skin from the edge of the hide. It should be a consistent blue-gray color all the way through. A double-check can be made by boiling the sliver of skin. A fully tanned piece will not curl or harden after it has boiled for a few minutes

If the skin is not completely tanned, return it to the solution for three more days. You can't leave it too long, but be sure it's ready before you take it out.

Rinse. Take the hide from the solution and rinse it well in clear water. Prepare a solution of one ounce bicarbonate of soda (baking soda) to one gallon of water. (Five gallons will probably be needed.) The skin can be washed in this solution for thirty minutes in an old wringer-type washing machine (if you can find one) or soaked in the solution for two hours, with frequent stirring.

When the hide is removed from the soda solution, rinse it thoroughly in clear water. Put the hide on the fleshing beam, slick it out on both sides, then stretch it out on the drying frame. The skin must be stretched tight but not over-stretched. This will weaken the leather. Stretching is generally accomplished by starting with a few hooks on each side and going around and around, restretching the sides.

Oiling. After stretching, and while the skin is still wet, put a liberal coat of warm *Neat's Foot Oil* on both sides, especially the flesh side.

Drying and Softening. Let the skin dry completely, then remove it from the frame and re-wet the skin. If a wringer washer is available the hide can be wrung out with the wringer, but it should not be twist-wrung by hand. If the leather slips on the wringers, fold a bath towel over the hide with the towel between the skin and the roller. As the skin dries, work it on the softening stake like shining shoes—back and forth. Every inch of the hide must be pulled over the sharp edge of the stake. This should be done every 15 to 30 minutes as the skin is drying. In between workings, hang the hide in the shade.

The flesh-side can be finished off with sandpaper or a sanding disk which will make a smooth, soft surface.

Chrome-tan leather is a blue-gray color when it is finished.

Acid Tanning

The hide is dehaired as previously described. Then mix a solution of one-half ounce of concentrated sulphuric acid (it can be bought at a pharmacy) or two ounces of sulphuric battery acid (it can be bought at an auto-parts house) to one pound of non-iodized salt and one gallon of water. The salt is dissolved first in the water, then the acid added. Be careful! Wear goggles and rubber gloves. Do not breathe fumes that transpire (a deadly mist) when the acid is added to the salt water. Stir gently as the acid is slowly added. (This solution must be mixed in a non-metalic container.) Place the neutralized skin in the solution. Let it soak for three days, stirring at least twice a day with the wooden stirring stick. Check the skin by cutting the hide in the thickest area and see if the white color of the acid tan goes all the way through the skin. If there is a flesh-appearing area in the middle put the skin back in the solution.

Depending on temperature it will generally take three days for a rabbit skin and six days for a deer hide to complete the acid process.

After finishing with the acid continue with the rinse, oiling, drying, and softening process described under chrome tanning.

Acid-tan leather is an off-white when it is finished.

Alum Tanning

Alum tanning requires either ammonium alum, potassium alum or aluminum sulfate. These alums are available at drug, grocery, and hardware stores. The aluminum sulfate can be purchased at garden supply stores.

Dehair and pickle as described previously. Then mix a solution of five pounds salt, two pounds alum or aluminum sulfate and ten gallons of water. Warm water should be used to stir in the ingredients or heated to assure that all solids are dissolved.

Let the solution cool before adding the skin, then let it soak for six days stirring at least twice a day.

The tan can be checked by slicing a sliver of leather from the edge of the skin. See if the white color is even through the hide. If it is not, return it to the solution.

After tanning, follow the same process of rinsing, oiling, drying, and softening as described under chrome tan.

Alum-tan leather is white when it is finished.

Vegetable Tanning

Ready-made vegetable tanning products are on the market under several brand names. Gambier, Sumac Extract, and Bark tan can be purchased from different supply houses. However, you can create your own vegetable tan solution from local plants. Any plant that has a high tannic acid content will work (i.e., oak bark, sumac bark, elderberry, walnut, and hemlock). Both the bark and the leaves are used. One pound of bark to one pound of skin is required.

The bark should be chipped as fine as possible then covered with water and simmered for three hours. As an alternative to simmering, the bark can be soaked in hot water for forty-eight hours.

The hide is dehaired and pickled then placed in the bark solution, whether commercial or homemade. Let it soak for two weeks and stir twice a day. The tan is checked by cutting a sliver from the edge of the hide. The color should be uniform all the way through. It will also pass the boiling test if it is tanned. If, after two weeks with homemade solution, the tan is not complete make a new solution and leave it in for another week.

The rinsing, oiling, drying, and softening is as described under chrome-tan.

Bark-tan leather is a brown color when it is finished.

Tanning Pelts

The process for tanning skins with the hair on is the same as what has already been described except that the step to dehair is omitted. The skin should be washed in Boraxo soap and then rinsed thoroughly before the tanning process is begun. When oiling is done be sure not to get oil on the fur side.

Dying Chrome Tan

Chrome-tan leather's blue-gray color will readily take a bark dye which will change it to brown. There are commercial dyes available which generally include the directions for their particular product. A homemade dye can be made from ten pounds of oak bark. Put the bark into a non-metallic container and pour boiling water over it. Let it set for two days then strain the liquid from the bark. Heat the liquid to a boil, let it cool, then soak the skin in it for twenty-four hours. Don't try to dye pelts with the hair still on unless you also want the hair colored.

Chapter 3

Making Rawhide

Early Indians developed the use of rawhide into a fine art. They used as many—if not more—rawhide articles than they did tanned articles. With rawhide they made cradles, drums, sunshades, knife sheaths, shields, toys, trunks, parfleche: thus rawhide became an important part of the buffalo culture.

Different animal skins produce rawhide with different qualities. Deerskin will make a pliable rawhide that works well for lacing anything that needs some give or twist to it after the rawhide is dry. Antelope rawhide is so thin and pliable it's almost worthless used as rawhide, but with very little work antelope rawhide can be made to be almost as soft as leather. Domestic cattle rawhide is stiff and hard which works well made into carrying cases to protect binoculars, etc. Elk falls somewhere between deer and cattle: it makes good knife sheaths.

Commercial rawhide is generally made from the hides of domestic cattle. It is very stiff and hard. It can be purchased in different thicknesses.

Rawhide Process

Plain Rawhide

To make rawhide, the hide is first dehaired as described in chapter 2. The epidermis is not removed (unless a soft, pliable rawhide is desired). After rinsing and cleaning, the hide is nailed to a wall, staked out on the ground, or placed on a drying frame. The hide should be dried in the shade to eliminate as much stress as possible. Rawhide shrinks a great deal and the faster it is dried the more it shrinks. If the finished product is to be shrunk to tighten, it should be dried in direct sunlight.

After the skin has completely dried it is removed and stored flat, or in a loose roll. Strips can be cut from this "sheet" and resoaked for lacing. Rawhide can be resoaked and redried several times. It will keep indefinitely as long as it is bone dry.

Oiled Rawhide

For oiled rawhide, the skin is dehaired leaving the epidermis unless a soft rawhide is desired. After rinsing, it is stretched out as described in making plain rawhide. While the hide is still wet, a light coat of oil is spread evenly over the grain—or hair—side of the skin. The end product is more resilient to water and can be used in areas where that quality is needed. If it is pounded, it is also a softer rawhide.

Again, store rawhide flat or in a loose roll and keep it dry.

Whitening and Softening Rawhide

The Indian people used a process of pounding to whiten and soften rawhide. The dry skin is placed on a bed of dry grass or some other padding. A hammer, the back of a single-bit axe, or a stone is then used to pound the flesh-side of the skin. This causes the hide to lose its transparent yellow color and turn white.

Areas that need to be flexible (such as a cover lid on a case) receive more pounding at the bend area. This breaks up the tissue to allow flexibility. Care must be taken not to "break" or damage the hide by a direct blow. Blows are struck at a glancing angle.

Sizing and Varnishing Rawhide

At some time in prehistory, Indian women found that if they applied a coat of "size" or "varnish" to their rawhide it resisted sun, air, and moisture.

Sizings included hide scrapings, fish roe (eggs), antler or horn glue, cactus juice, the lymph from a fish, wax from the tail of a beaver, or liquid from animal eyes. Varnish was made from different tree resins.

Prickly pear cactus is the most common material used for sizing. The cactus pad can be peeled (before pad is cut from the plant to avoid handling the spines), and the inner core rubbed on the flesh-side of the partly dry rawhide. When it is dry it will have a glossy finish.

Another method is to peel and boil the cactus pads and use the liquid to size the rawhide.

Chapter 4

Leather Working

Tools

Tools available for working leather are numerous, to say the least. Tandy Leather Company puts out a catalog with one section devoted wholly to stamps and punches. But don't feel you have to run out and buy every tool: You'll just become broke, nervous, and confused.

There are a few basic tools needed to get started, then your tool chest can grow as you go on in the world of leather.

Measuring and Cutting Tools

The beginning of any leather project is measuring and cutting.

Metal Square: A versatile measuring tool is a metal square (carpenter square). It allows a straight measure, a straight cutting edge, and a square corner or 90-degree vertical. It can be purchased at a lumber yard or any place that carries carpenter tools.

Metal Yardstick: If a metal square cannot be found, a metal yardstick is next best. It gives a good, straight edge to run your knife along. A wooden yardstick will get nicked up and cut with use.

Cutting Board: A 24-inch by 26-inch piece of plywood covered with artist matte board works well for a cutting board. Replace the matte board when it becomes too cut up.

Skife Knife: The skife is used to thin or "skive" leather. It uses replaceable injection blades so the knife needs no sharpening. The blade is so designed that you can't gouge the leather by cutting too deeply.

Utility Knife: A utility knife works well for all types of cutting except soft leather. It also has replaceable blades.

Shears: While special scissors can be bought for leather, any heavy pair will do. They are used for cutting soft leather and thin rawhide.

Tin Snips or Bezel Shears: Will also work to cut leather.

Draw-gauge: Although you can, with practice and experience, cut uniform strips of leather for lacing and belts it is done much easier with a draw-gauge. If you buy one, make sure it is heavy-duty metal.

Hammers and Punches

A punch or awl is a necessity for making holes for stitching or lacing in heavy leather. You can get by with a simple awl to start with. The four-prong and other specialized punches listed, however, make the job easier.

Four-prong Stitching Punch: This punch makes uniformly spaced holes for stitching heavy leather. It is punched with a hammer.

Rotary Punch: This is the most used punch tool you'll have: it is a tool you must have. This pliers-type tool contains six hollow tubes of varying sizes for different-size holes.

Miscellaneous Punches: A round punch in different sizes is used for extremely heavy leather. It makes the same hole as the rotary punch, but the round punch can be driven through heavier material. Punches also come in oblong and oval sizes. The oblong can be useful to make a hole for a strap such as on a sandal. Both come in varying sizes.

Rawhide Mallet: The mallet is used to hit the prong punches through the leather. It can also be useful in setting snaps, etc.

Ball-peen Hammer: The metal ball-peen hammer is used to flatten rivets and for heavy punch work. The rounded end will also work to whiten rawhide.

Wooden Punch Block: Any piece of wood—but preferably hardwood—for placing under the leather you are going to punch. A hardwood-tree block, at table height, works very well.

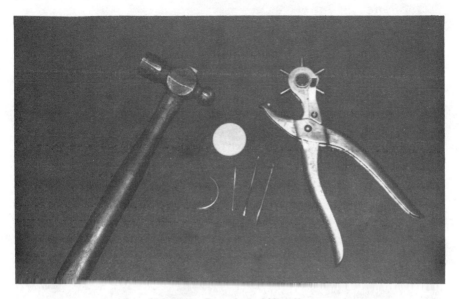

Hammer, Punch and Needles
Left to right: ball-peen hammer; I.V. rubber needle puller; rotary leather punch; assorted needles used in sewing leather.

Stitching Tools

Harness Needle: Used to sew waxed thread through pre-punched holes. It is available in a variety of sizes.

Glover's Needle: A three-cornered needle used to sew lightweight leather without pre-punching.

Lock-stitch Sewing Awl: This is a basic hand-sewing machine that does a locking stitch by hand. It is very useful on heavy leather. It can be used as an awl to poke holes but the needles are not as sturdy as an awl should be.

Pliers: Although you can buy a special lacing plier, any needle-nose type will do. They are used to help pull the needle through heavy leather.

The rubber seal on an I.V. bottle is about one inch in diameter by 1/16-of-an-inch thick and works well to grip the needle to be pushed or pulled through leather. The seal does not break as many needles as the pliers do. Nurses throw them away so if you know someone working at a hospital, stock up—the discards are free.

Miscellaneous Tools

Ruffer: A ruffer is used to give a rough surface on smooth leather for gluing.

Snap Setter: Used for setting snaps. A must if you are going to use snaps.

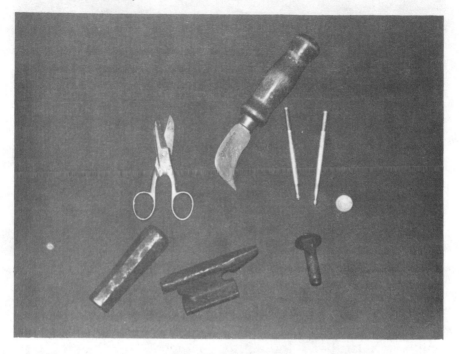

Miscellaneous Tools

Top (left to right): telephone repairman shears; carpet knife; snap setters with base. Bottom (left to right): two styles of metal anvils for riveting and setting snaps; rivet tool to start the rounding of the pin over the washer. Made from a carriage bolt drilled in the end to form the needed cup.

Miscellaneous Supplies

Waxed Thread: Comes in black, natural, and brown, and is available in a variety of thicknesses. It can be used with the lock-stitch sewing awl.

Rubber Cement: Shoe-supply rubber cement is the best. It can be bought by the quart. Get some thinner while you're at it since it seems that glue is always being left to congeal into a "blob."

Rivets: There are many different kinds of rivets. You'll need to check to decide what is best for the job. Some points to keep in mind while shopping are: copper rivets turn green with age and use but do not rust; iron rivets rust if used in a damp setting. The shaft of the rivet must not be too long or too short for the thickness of leather that is being joined. Rivets come in two parts; the male and the female, or washer. You must have both parts to get the job done.

Sandpaper: Sandpaper is needed for smoothing out home-tanned leather and cut edges of store-bought leather.

Pattern Paper: Newsprint ends make an inexpensive pattern paper, but they tend to tear. Large brown-paper grocery sacks work well and don't tear as easily. If they are not available, brown wrapping paper can be bought.

Hardware

For each product you are going to create there will be a need for rings, buckles, snaps, etc. A local supply house will carry a large variety. Some "D" rings and larger hardware can be found at a horse tack outlet.

It is handy to keep a supply of snaps and rivets on hand to make repairs and to build something on the spur of the moment.

Leather-Working Techniques

Cutting

Draw the pattern on paper, cut it out, then tape it with masking tape to the leather. Light-weight leather is cut along the pattern with shears in the same way cloth is cut. Heavy-weight leather must be placed on the cutting board on the floor and cut with a utility knife.

Place the metal straight-edge, either the square or the yardstick, along the line to be cut. Put your knee on one end of the straight-edge and your free hand on the other end, then draw the knife along the edge. (Always get out of the way when the knife is coming at you!)

Curves and the like must be freehanded. It will get easier as time goes on, believe it or not.

Lacing: Cutting lacing can be done easily with a draw-gauge, but, should you not want to buy one right now, don't despair.

Place a sharp-bladed knife, point first, in a heavy block of wood. Take the leather to be made into lacing in both hands. Slowly—with an up motion—pull the leather into the sharp blade. (With a little practice the lacing will be uniform in width.) Make the cut around the outer edge of the leather going in a circle. By using this technique the lacing can be cut as long as is needed.

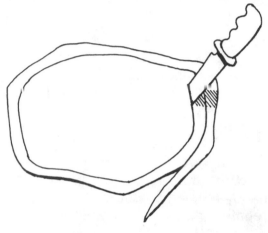

Cutting Lacing

This same method can be used to get lacing from deer-skin rawhide, although often it can be cut with shears just as easily.

Shaping Leather and Rawhide

Many articles can be made by shaping wet leather or rawhide and letting it dry to the desired shape: Hats, bowls, carry-jugs are just a few of these articles.

Leather to be shaped must be vegetable-tan leather. Both leather and rawhide are shaped under the same process.

A form is built in the shape desired for the finished product. Keep in mind that the leather and rawhide, especially the rawhide, will shrink around the form. The form must be designed so the material can be removed when the leather has shrunk and has become hard or stiff.

The leather—or rawhide—is thoroughly soaked in water until saturated, then shaped over the form with your hands. When the desired shape and smoothness is obtained, the material is fastened in place by nails. On some shapes, the form can be cut from the center of a wood piece allowing the outer wood to be slipped back over the center piece after the material is in place. This will hold it without nails. In the case of rawhide, great care must be taken to anchor it firmly because of its shrinking characteristic.

If the item is to be laced with rawhide or leather, all lacing must be done while the article is still wet.

The material is left in place until totally dry, then removed from the form. The edges can then be trimmed and buffed.

Sewing and Stitches

Running Stitch: This simple stitch, over and under, is not strong and will tend to "draw" or "pucker" but it is easy and quick to fasten two overlapped pieces.

Saddlestitch: The saddlestitch is a very strong stitch. It is actually the running stitch run back over itself. First do a running stitch the length of the area to be sewn. Now, reverse and go the opposite direction so the finished product looks like a continuous stitch, not the every-other-one look of the running stitch. At the end use two needles, one for each end of the thread on opposite sides of the material. To tie it off sew them back over the stitches with about four stitches coming into the same hole from opposite sides.

Whip Stitch: This is a simple edge stitch. It is used when the materials are placed side by side, exposing two raw edges. The stitching goes over the edges of the material that is becoming decorative. This is not a strong stitch. It is sewed back through itself to tie off.

Cross Stitch: Cross stitch is the strongest edge stitch. It is the whip stitch doubled back on itself or by skipping every other hole going one way and hitting those holes on the way back.

Rawhide Lacing: The rawhide must be thoroughly soaked and laced wet, pulling as tight as possible. If a knot is tied in the rawhide lacing, the loose ends of the knot must be held by

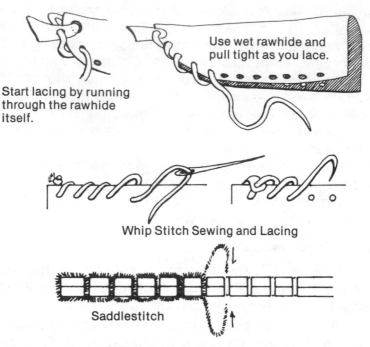

Start lacing by running through the rawhide itself.

Use wet rawhide and pull tight as you lace.

Whip Stitch Sewing and Lacing

Saddlestitch

Stitches & Rawhide Lacing

placing straight pins—or small nails—through them as close to the knot as possible and left until completely dry or they will pull through and untie.

When lacing hides with the hair on, pull the hair back on top after the lacing has pulled it down so the lacing can be hidden under the hair. The hair is pulled out with an awl.

Rawhide lacing will shrink and tighten as it dries and can cause the material to pucker. This can be prevented by fastening the article in the desired shape while the lacing dries.

A whip stitch is generally used for rawhide lacing.

Other Fasteners

Snaps and Velcro tape are easily worked into leather articles. Velcro becomes only a method of fastening while snaps can be part of the decorative design.

Both snaps and Velcro come in a variety of sizes. Snaps require a snap-setting tool the right size for the right snap and a punch to make the right size hole. Tandy Leather Company

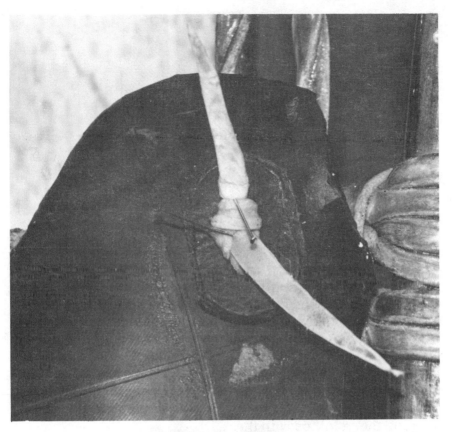

Pinning Wet Rawhide Knots
Straight pins are placed through the wet rawhide lacing after the knot is tied as close to the knot as possible to prevent the knot from untying while the rawhide dries and shrinks.

carries all you'll need for snaps. Fabric shops carry the Velcro tape.

Buttons and toggle-fasteners can be made from elk or deer antlers. Toggles can be made from teeth although they tend to crack and break after a few years (except for elk eye-teeth).

Leather lacing wrapped on antler buttons makes a quick and easy fastener.

Beadwork, Quillwork, Bells, and Fringe

The culture of a people has always been expressed in their art and clothing. Early Indians had work clothing which,

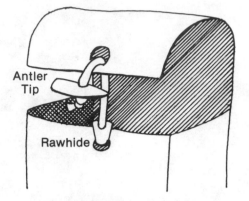

Toggle Fastener

other than the loin cloth, was not worn often except when weather conditions required. These items of clothing were plain, created to meet a need and to be practical. Their ceremonial dress clothes were worn during many types of ceremonies. The men's dress shirts (called "war shirts") were worn during battle. They wore their best to war although they stripped down to do the actual fighting.

It was the dress clothes that reflected their culture. They were covered with quillwork, feathers, ermine tails, hair and fringe. After the glass bead was brought to them the Indians adorned their clothes with them.

It brings pride to make your own clothing no matter how it looks, but it is a special exhilarated pride when the clothing is also your work through the art of beading, fringing, or quilling.

Beadwork

Beadwork gives culture, beauty and uniqueness to leather creation. Early Indians developed beadwork to a fine art after the white man brought trade beads. Because the plains Indians were using porcupine quills before they used trade beads most of their designs were block and geometric, the easiest design created with quills. Their beadwork followed the same basic designs.

Missionaries brought floral designs and some Indian people followed those patterns.

Imagination is the only limit to your creative beadwork.

Loom beading is the easiest and most common method. The first rule in loom beading is to select the beads. Mill-run beads tend to look very rough on the finished product because of their varied sizes and shapes. They even have different-size holes which places them differently on the warp threads. Go through the purchased beads you have and pick those of uniform size and shape as much as possible before you begin your project.

Looms may be purchased at craft shops but they tend to be too short which makes creating a long bead strip more complicated. A loom may be made very easily and can be made to be adjustable.

Some tribes used a box loom. This allowed wide weaving for wide bead-bands used for pouches and bags. As illustrated, the sides of a box loom must be below—and wider than—the warp thread to allow beading without the sides being in the way.

Most Indian work is sewn directly to the article to be beaded as the beading takes place. This is more complicated to do but it gives a smoother-finished appearance.

Monofiliment fishline works well for the warp thread. Any strong thread will work, such as buttonhole thread. The weaving—or weft thread—must be a diameter that can go through the bead hole and allow the beading needle to pass back through the bead with the thread in it. If the thread is too large the bead will break on the second pass through with the needle. At the same time, the thread must be strong. A broken bead means undoing all that has been done back to that point to replace it. Use good-quality beads and be sure the hole will accept your thread and needle twice.

At the same time, if you find you need to break a bead out of the middle of the string, pushing an over-size needle or awl in the hole will do it. Needle nose pliers can also be used to break the bead, but this should be done so as not to put pressure on the weft thread.

Beads are placed according to color in different containers. Shallow bowls work well. It's better not to mix colors. This will prevent getting a wrong color later when you are stringing.

The warp thread is wrapped on the desired loom, as illustrated. Weft thread is woven on the warp thread three or four

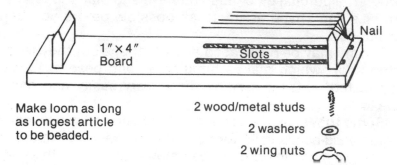

1/16″ Notches for String Spacing

1″ × 4″ Board

Slots

Nail

Make loom as long
as longest article
to be beaded.

2 wood/metal studs

2 washers

2 wing nuts

Homemade Adjustable Bead Loom

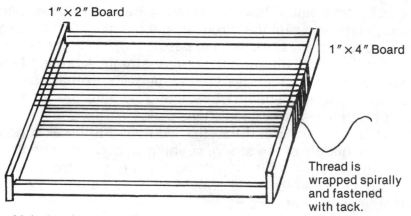

1″ × 2″ Board

1″ × 4″ Board

Thread is
wrapped spirally
and fastened
with tack.

Make box loom as wide and long as needed.

Box Bead Loom

times before the beading begins. A knot is tied on one side of the warp threads in the weft thread and the threads pulled up tight. (See illustration.)

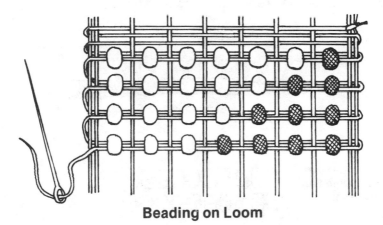

Beading on Loom

The desired color combination and the number of beads needed to make your pattern are placed on the weft thread with the needle pulled tight and pushed into the warp threads with the index finger of the left hand. Hold the beads up in place with the index finger of the left hand while the needle is passed back through the beads with the right hand. This places the weft thread on top of the warp thread. (If you are left-handed reverse the order.) This process is continued until the pattern is complete.

When the weaving is finished, weave several weft threads as was done in the beginning and tie It off. Make sure all warp threads are tied off. If all knots are tied on the top as you work, the article can be turned over when it is finished. With all the knots on the bottom they won't show.

Draw the pattern on paper first. Graph paper works well. Count the number of beads of each color you plan to use and graph which weave they will go into.

Loom beading should be sewn onto a cloth backing before it is put on leather since leather tends to stretch as it is used and stretching will break the threads that hold the beads. If the beading is placed on a cloth backing this shouldn't happen.

Sewing beads directly onto the material to be beaded is more complicated but it makes a better product. The pattern is drawn on graph paper and transferred to the material to be beaded. The beads are stitched as illustrated.

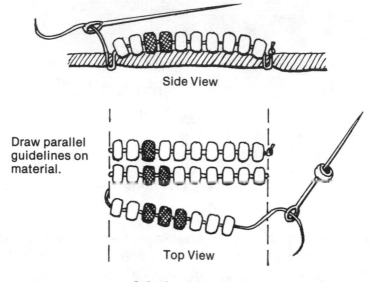

Side View

Draw parallel guidelines on material.

Top View

Stitched Beading

A frame must be made to place the material on to sew the beads directly to it. Embroidery hoops can be used or a wooden frame made from a wood soft enough that the leather can be fastened to it with tacks.

1" × 2" Board

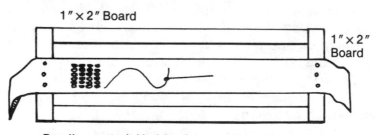

1" × 2" Board

Beading material held to frame with tacks.
Make frame the size needed.

Bead Stitching Frame

Quillwork

Quills from porcupines were the decorating medium of the plains Indians before they had trade beads. If you are fortunate enough to live in an area where the porcupine lives, road-kills will generally keep you supplied in quills.

The quills are pulled from the carcass carefully to avoid having yourself become their victim. The quills are sorted by size. The smaller, fine ones come from the upper belly and neck; larger, course quills come from the back. There are small quills throughout the porky's body.

Start the process by soaking the quills in clear water. They are then boiled in dye, but just for a short time so as not to over-soften the quill. Early Indians used plant dyes such as squawberry for red; curlydock root for pastel yellow; stinging nettle root for yellow. Commercial dyes can also be used. When the quills have reached the desired color they are set on a log, or board, to dry.

The quills are held in the mouth to soften and prepare them for flattening and wrapping. There are four uses of quills: wrapping, braiding or plaiting, weaving, and sewing. Wrapping is the easiest to do.

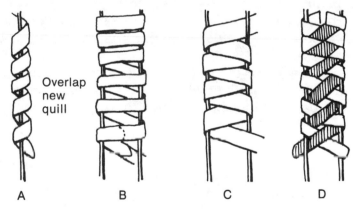

Overlap new quill

A   B   C   D

Stitch finished "threads" to article to be decorated.

    A. Quill on single string
    B. One quill applied straight on two threads
    C. One quill weaved on two threads
    D. Two quills weaved on two threads

Quillwork

The quill is flattened with your thumbnail or by being pulled through your teeth. It can be flattened more by using a burnishing tool. The tool is made of a smoothly polished flat bone, usually a deer foreleg. Commercial burnishing tools can be purchased at any drafting supply store.

The quill is then wrapped around a piece of fringe, thread, or two pieces of thread 1/8-inch apart. The pattern must be drawn out and planned similar to what is done for beadwork.

After the pattern and design are completed and wrapped the quillwork is sewn to the article it is to beautify.

Bells

Small bells of all kinds and shapes can be used to enhance the appearance of a leather garment. They are generally attached to the fringe with string, thread, or sinew. They can be sown dirootly to the clothing williuul uslriy frlnge.

Fringe

Fringe was the trademark of the plains Indians. Ceremonial clothes had fringe dragging the ground and so thick that those wearing it could not walk through brush. Fringe adds beauty and grace to leather clothing.

Fringe can be cut by leaving extra leather on the article for that purpose, or by sewing extra leather in the seams of the shirts, dresses and leggings. The narrower the fringe is cut—and the softer the leather it is cut from—the more attractive the finished product will be. Your imagination is the limit to what can be done with fringe to spice up your clothing.

Chapter 5

Leather Makings

Clothing

All articles of clothing should be made from a pattern first made on paper. The illustrations will show what measurements are needed and how to make the item. The text will tell how many hides, if any, are needed and what kind of leather will give the most satisfactory product.

Shirt: The easiest to make and most practical leather shirt to wear is like those worn by the early Paiutes. This shirt requires three average-size mule deerskins to make if it has long sleeves, two hides if it has short sleeves. Deer or antelope should be used because of their soft leather. If you are buying commercial leather, any soft, two-ounce chrome-tanned leather will work.

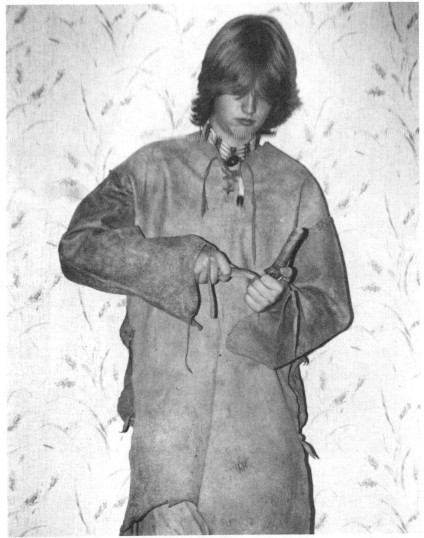

Leather Work Shirt
(Paiute Pattern)

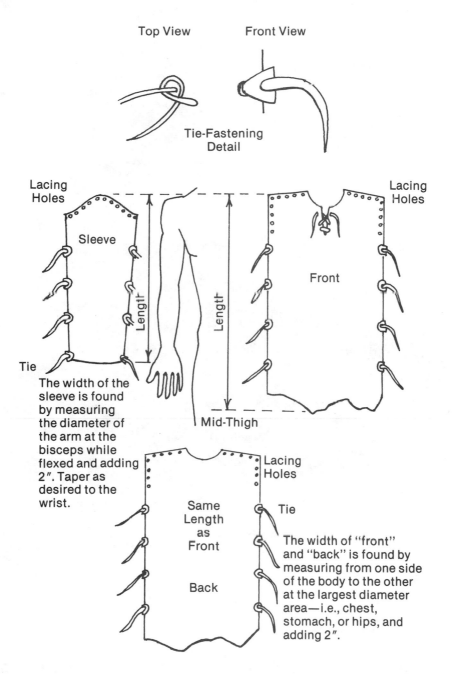

Top View   Front View

Tie-Fastening
Detail

Lacing Holes

Sleeve

Lacing Holes

Front

Length   Length

Tie

The width of the sleeve is found by measuring the diameter of the arm at the biceps while flexed and adding 2″. Taper as desired to the wrist.

Mid-Thigh

Same Length as Front

Lacing Holes

Tie

Back

The width of "front" and "back" is found by measuring from one side of the body to the other at the largest diameter area—i.e., chest, stomach, or hips, and adding 2″.

Paiute Shirt Pattern

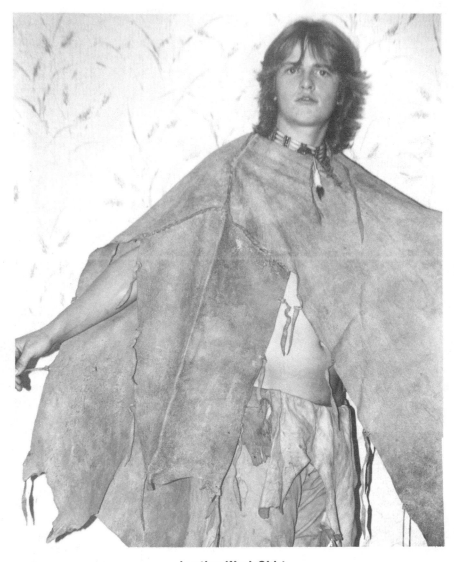

Leather Work Shirt
(Paiute Pattern)
The shirt is untied and opened to be used as a poncho.

Loincloth: A loincloth should be made from a 3-foot-by-1-foot piece of chamois or a split chrome-tan leather. The leather-tie belt should be about two inches wide and strong enough to hold leggings, if need be. The length depends on waist size of the wearer.

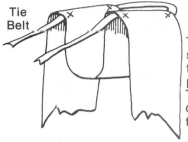

The loin cloth can be stitched to the tie belt at the "X" to help keep it in position when wearing. The "X" location must be determined while wearing the loin cloth.

Loincloth

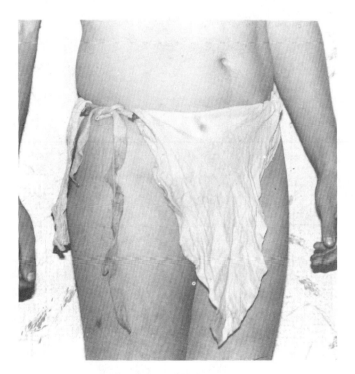

Loincloth

Leggings: One average-size mule deerskin will make a pair of leggings for an average-size man. A soft two-ounce chrome-tan leather should be used. It can be dyed, or be a combination chrome-and-vegetable-tan but it should have the chrome tan to withstand repeated wetting.

Leggings with Loin Cloth

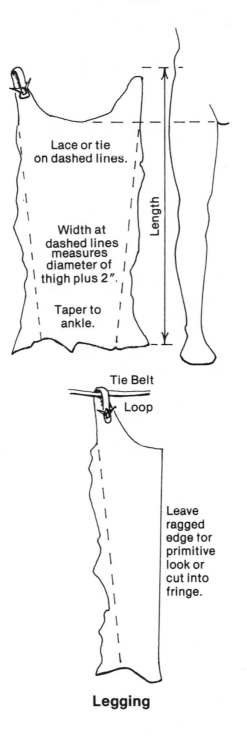

Lace or tie on dashed lines.

Length

Width at dashed lines measures diameter of thigh plus 2″.

Taper to ankle.

Tie Belt

Loop

Leave ragged edge for primitive look or cut into fringe.

Legging

Dress: Two elk or three mule deerskins are required for a dress. It is important to obtain a light two-ounce, yet strong, chrome-tan leather for this item. Because of the bulk of material needed it can become too heavy for comfort.

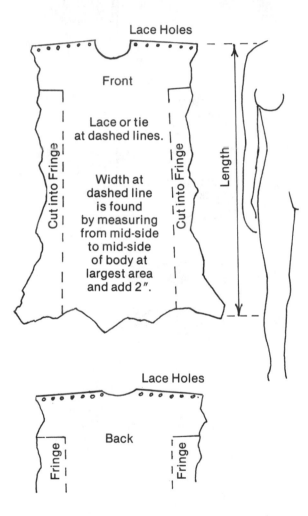

Work Dress Pattern

Leather Work Dress

Mittens: The outer mitten should be of a chrome-tan or oil-tan material. If they are to receive lots of wear the mittens should be made from oil tan. The inner mitten, or liners, are generally chrome-tanned rabbit. The fur is turned in.

If one-piece construction is wanted, chrome-tan sheepskin works well with the wool turned inside. About three square feet are needed for an average-sized man.

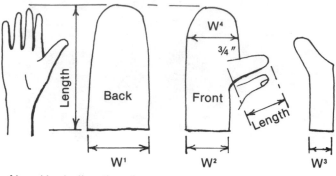

W¹ = width of hand including thumb
W² = ⅔ W¹
W³ = ⅓ W¹
W⁴ = same width as back
Allow additional ½" all around for seams
If using sheepskin with wool inside, add for thickness of wool.

Mitten

Muff: Rabbit and/or beaver and/or sheepskin make good muffs. It requires a piece two feet by one foot to make either the liner or the outer covering. Because of their exposure to moisture in the winter, they should be chrome tanned. A combination of skins can be used with one for the liner and another for the outer. The fur is turned in for the liner and out for the covering.

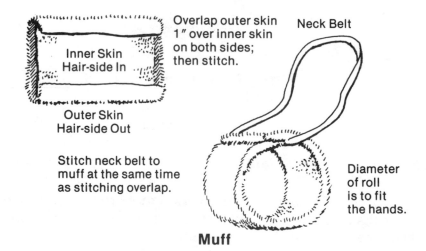

Inner Skin
Hair-side In

Outer Skin
Hair-side Out

Overlap outer skin
1" over inner skin
on both sides;
then stitch.

Neck Belt

Stitch neck belt to
muff at the same time
as stitching overlap.

Diameter
of roll
is to fit
the hands.

Muff

Rabbitskin Muff

Belt: Belts should be made from vegetable tan if they are to be tooled. Mountain-man belts can be made from any type of tan depending on the desired effect.

Winter Face Mask: Chrome-tanned rabbit is best for face masks. The hair is turned in and the areas around the eyes, nose, and mouth shaved to prevent icing. One rabbit skin is needed per mask.

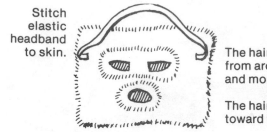

Stitch elastic headband to skin.

The hair is trimmed from around the eyes and mouth as shown.

The hair-side is worn toward the face.

Rabbitskin Winter Face Mask

Elkskin Robe: One elk hide tanned with the hair on is needed for a robe. It can be any type tan but it must be a soft tan. Lacing and a fastener are required to tie the robe on.

Elkskin Robe

Elkskin Robe

Hats

Formed Leather Hat: Vegetable tan is a must for a formed hat. It requires a three-foot-square piece of leather. A wooden, or styrofoam, form is made in the desired shape. The leather is soaked, stretched over the form, then tacked in place until dry.

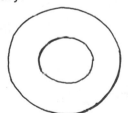

Cut brim to desired size and lace or stitch to hat. The brim can be one piece or several pieces stitched together.

a = ⅓ diameter of head plus 1″.

Stitch 3 leather triangles together after fitting on head or form. Wet and stretch onto form. Tack at base and leave until dry.

Formed Hat

Fur Hat: Chrome tan is needed to guard against sweating and other moisture a fur cap might be subjected to. Almost any type of animal skin can be used according to personal taste. One skin the size of a raccoon or badger skin is required.

The head is cut off and stitched onto the front of finished hat.

Using the front and back leg fold over tucking the edge of the belly under to form hat. Cut where necessary to take out folds. Stitch in place pulling the hair over to hide the stitches.

Fur Hat

Visor: The visor must be made from a stiff combination tan (vegetable/chrome). One square foot of leather is required.

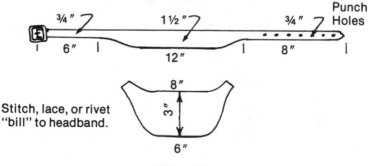

Punch Holes

¾ "   1½ "   ¾ "

6"   12"   8"

Stitch, lace, or rivet "bill" to headband.

8"

3"

6"

Visor Hat

Fur Hat
Badger-skin hat with rabbitskin liner. One-piece construction pattern.

Leather Visor

Footwear

Moccasins: Moccasins should be made from deerskin or elk skin with a rawhide, or Latigo, sole. Several pair can be made from one hide. A two- to four-ounce chrome-tan leather is best if bought commercially because of repeated wettings. About four square feet are required for the pattern illustrated.

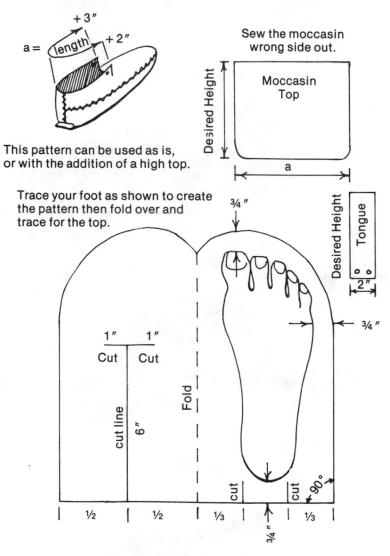

Nez Perce-Flathead Pattern

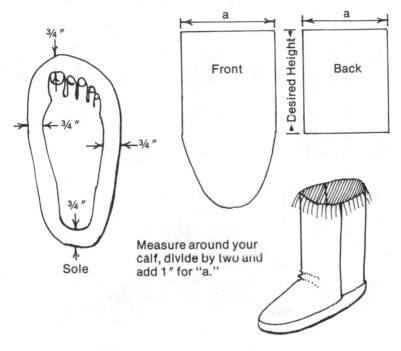

Measure around your calf, divide by two and add 1″ for "a."

Apache Pattern

A heavy sole may be stitched onto the finished moccasin. Use the Apache sole pattern.

Nez Perce-Flathead with Top and Tongue

Moccasins
Left to right: Apache boot pattern; Nez Perce-Flathead pattern on "Cabbage Patch"; Nez Perce-Flathead pattern with additional heavy sole.

Sandals: Sandals are made from Latigo and sole leather. There are many designs and patterns for sandals but those illustrated are practical and simple to make. One square foot of sole leather and one square foot of Latigo are required for the pattern shown.

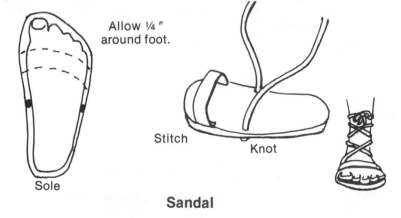

Allow ¼ " around foot.

Sole

Stitch

Knot

Sandal

Mukluks: Mukluks require chrome-tan sheepskin and Latigo for a sole. Lacing is made from chrome-tan deer or oil-tan soft leather of any kind. One average-size sheepskin will make one pair of high-top mukluks. Two square feet of Latigo are required for the soles and eight feet of half-inch lacing. Indoor-outdoor carpet works well for a bottom insole. A felt insole, or an insole made from sheepskin with wool, is placed on top of the indoor-outdoor carpet.

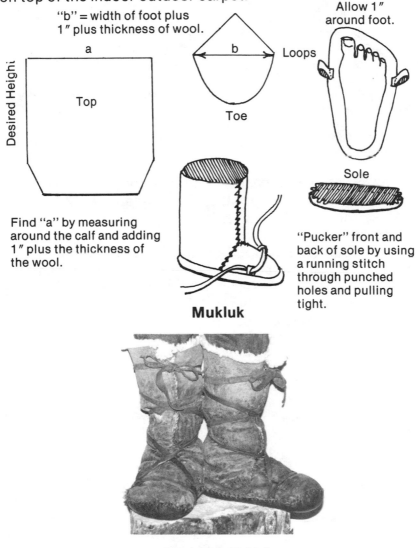

"b" = width of foot plus 1" plus thickness of wool.

Desired Height

a

Top

Allow 1" around foot.

b

Loops

Toe

Sole

Find "a" by measuring around the calf and adding 1" plus the thickness of the wool.

"Pucker" front and back of sole by using a running stitch through punched holes and pulling tight.

Mukluk

Sheepskin Mukluks

Rabbit-skin Liners: Rabbit-skin liners are constructed from fresh wild, or domestic, rabbit hides. It requires one hide for one liner.

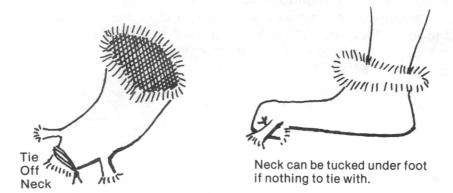

Tie Off Neck

Neck can be tucked under foot if nothing to tie with.

Rabbit-skin Liner

The skin must be cased-skinned with as little blood as possible getting on the fur side of the hide. The skin is then turned so that the hair is inside. The neck area is tied shut with a piece of cord, or it can be folded over if no string is available. The hide is placed on the foot and a sock pulled over the skin and the foot, then the boot is put on. The skin will dry as the person walks, which works the skin to softness in the areas that must be soft.

If the skin is not dry at bedtime they must be worn to bed because they will shrink and become too stiff to wear if left out to dry.

Baby Carriers

Rawhide Infant Carrier: Deerskin rawhide is the easiest to work with for this project. The carrier should be made large enough to last until the baby can hold up its head—at about three months.

The carrier is made of two pieces of rawhide cut to the patterns. The end section is laced on as illustrated using either rawhide lacing or a leather thong. To hold the baby in the lacing must be soft leather. The carrier should be lined with cloth or with soft rabbit skins.

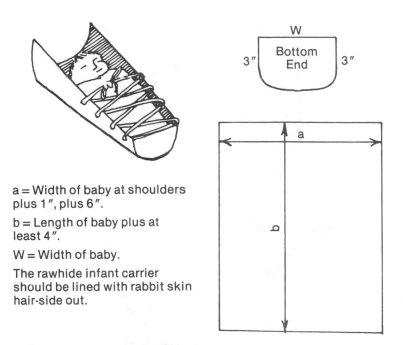

a = Width of baby at shoulders plus 1″, plus 6″.

b = Length of baby plus at least 4″.

W = Width of baby.

The rawhide infant carrier should be lined with rabbit skin hair-side out.

Rawhide Infant Carrier

Cradleboard: One deerskin is needed to make a cradle-board. The leather should be a soft tan. The frame can be made from willow, ash, or any soft—yet strong—wood. It is best to get the wood and make the frame in the spring, but with proper soaking or the use of steam it can be made any time.

The wood is shaped to the desired shape and size and staked on the ground to dry (see illustration). Wrapping the separate sections together with cloth or leather helps maintain the form while it is drying.

When the outside frame is completed, a platform is lashed to the frame for the baby to lay on. The willow frame is best suited for a summer packboard because it allows air to circulate on the baby's back. A piece of 3/8-inch plywood cut in the same shape as the willow frame can be used for a winter cradleboard. This keeps the warmth in. Padding such as rabbit skin or cloth should be placed between the youngster and the platform, or plywood.

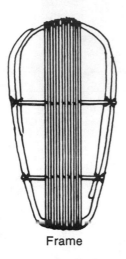

Frame

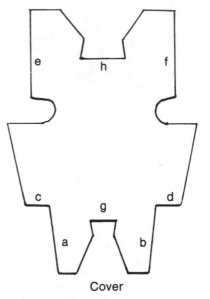

Cover

Sew "a" to "b," "c" to "d" and "e" to "f."

Cover must be measured to fit size of frame.

Sew cover, then slip on frame.

Frame should be at least 12" longer than child— 8" above and 4" at bottom.

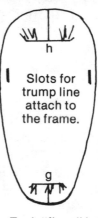

Slots for trump line attach to the frame.

Tuck "flaps" into back and sew.

Cradleboard

Cradleboard Frame
The green limbs are held in place with stakes and rock while drying in the desired shape.

Cradleboard
Finished cradleboard for a three-to-six-month-old child.

When the frame is completed, the deerskin is cut to the pattern and sewed together on the frame. It may be decorated with beads, bells, and fringe, or left plain. The lacing to hold the baby in should be started in the middle of the cover and laced in both directions for the ease of placing the child in the leather. Leather for the lacing should be a soft tan.

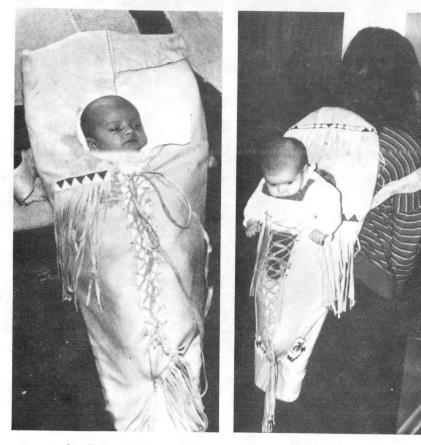

Cradleboard Wrap
Young baby wrapped in cradleboard. Child must be able to support his own head before he can be placed in a cradleboard.

Cradleboard Carry
Older child laced in a cradleboard being carried with a trumpline.

Toddler's Packsack: One deerskin is needed to make a toddler packsack. It should be medium softness. Any tan will work but chrome tan is preferred because of its ability to be washed and retain softness after repeated wettings.

Shoulder straps can be made from leather, or commercial straps may be purchased from mountaineering shops and adapted to the pack. Belts—both webbing and leather—can be bought at thrift stores and used for shoulder straps also.

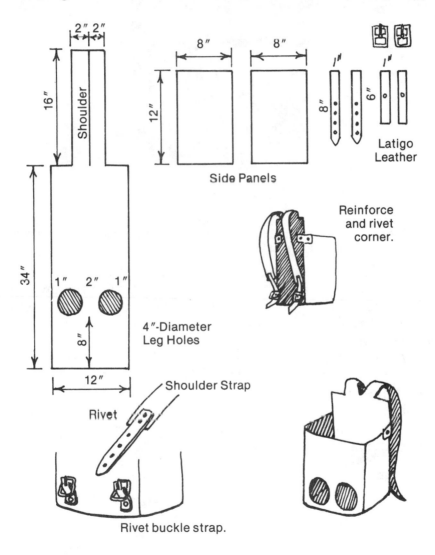

Toddler's Packsack

Toddler's Packsack
The leather toddler packsack can be attached to a metal frame or made with its own shoulder straps as this one is.

The pack is constructed as illustrated and leg holes cut in the bottom. It should be made deep enough to allow the child to go to sleep (as they often do when being packed) and have support without their head hanging over the edge which chokes them.

Another method is to make a toddler pack and attach straps that allow the pack to be fastened to a commercial pack frame. For long-distance packing this is the most comfortable route to go.

A pack frame can be constructed from wood but, if it is, weight quickly becomes a problem.

Water Carriers

Emergency Skin Canteen: In an emergency, raw skin of a rabbit or any animal can be used for a short time to carry water. To make a permanent canteen use a vegetable-tan stiff six- to nine-ounce weight. Leather that can be shaped and waxed will give the best product. The amount of leather needed depends on the size of the canteen that will be made.

Tie with thong
after filling with water.
Leave a carry loop.

Hair-Side Out

Tie off front legs.

Tie the neck, double over
and tie again.

Emergency Skin Canteen

The vegetable-tanned leather is soaked and shaped over a form made out of wood as discussed in the chapter 4 section on "Shaping Leather and Rawhide."

½ diameter to fit a cork.

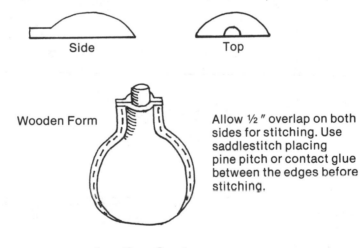

Side   Top

Wooden Form

Allow ½ " overlap on both sides for stitching. Use saddlestitch placing pine pitch or contact glue between the edges before stitching.

Leather Canteen

Once the product has been formed, it is stitched together. Surfaces to be stitched can be sealed with conifer tree pitch such as pine before it is stitched. The seams are waxed and the entire surface waxed and polished when the product is finished.

Bottle Cover: Vegetable-tanned leather of a stiff six- to nine-ounce weight is used for bottle covers. A bottle with a uniform, smooth shape is required, such as a standard wine bottle.

Soak the leather and form it around the bottle leaving a one-inch edge for seams. The seams are sown while the leather is wet and then let dry on the bottle. The outside can be waxed after it is dry. The bottle is left in the leather.

Dishes

Shaped Leather: Dishes are made from a six- to nine-ounce vegetable-tan leather. A mold the desired shape of the container must be made first (normally from wood). The leather is then soaked and stretched over the form as discussed in chapter 4. After drying, the edges are trimmed and sanded. The outside surface can be waxed.

Rawhide: Dishes are formed from any stiff rawhide such as domestic cattle rawhide. The wet, oiled skin is stretched over a form, preferably wood, although existing containers can be used if there is a method of tacking the skin while it is drying.

The edges should be trimmed as much as possible before it is dry. After the hide dries, it's time for the final trim and sanding of the edges. The finished product can be painted with designs using acrylic paint. Commercial varnish can be painted over the finished design or sizing from cactus as discussed in the chapter 3 section on "Sizing and Varnishing Rawhide."

Bedding

Rabbit-skin Blanket: Wild, untanned rabbit skins (preferably blacktailed jack rabbit hides) are used to make this early Indian blanket.

The rabbit is case-skinned and all flesh and fat removed from the hide. Put a knife in a stump as described in cutting lacing. Next the skin is cut in a continuous, one-inch-wide strip, by spiraling around the body. After cutting into a long, continuous strip the end of the strip is held on the ground with one foot and the other end held in the air by one hand. It is twirled until only hair is showing (do not over-twist or it will weaken the skin). The strips are hung straight to dry. It takes fifty skins to make a single adult blanket.

Rabbit-skin Blanket

Cutting a "cased-skinned" rabbit hide into strips for a blanket. The same method can be used to cut leather lacing.

The rabbit-skin strip is then twisted or twirled by holding one end with a foot and twirling the other end with your hand.

After the skins are dry, tie a double cord, head high, between two objects. The length of this string will be a foot wider
than the width of the desired blanket. Tie the cords together
on one end then tightly twine the rabbit-skin strips between
them. When all the strips are twined into the cords, the other
end of the cord is also fastened head high.

Cordage is now twined across the width of the strips
every twelve inches continuing down the "blanket" with one
twining placed three inches from the bottom.

This blanket will shed rabbit hair continually, but it is
attractive and warm.

*Cordage is twined into the rabbit-skin strips by weaving two cords over and
under the strip.*

The cordage is twined every twelve inches for the length of the rabbit-skin strips which will form the blanket.

Patchwork Blanket: This blanket is generally made from tanned rabbit skins although any fur-bearing animal skin can be used.

The tanned hides are cut to fit and patched together in the same way a patchwork quilt is done. It can be a solid color or made in a mosaic design. The flesh-side can be lined with cloth material or left open to the leather. Chrome tan allows the blanket to be washed if needed. All skins used should be a soft tan.

Carry Bags

Medicine Bag: The simplest medicine bag is constructed from the scrotum of an animal. It can be tanned, or simply oiled and worked rawhide.

The scrotum doesn't have to be sewed or cut, only tied together at the top. A long cord can be used so the bag can be hung around the neck or the cord cut off and the bag carried in a pocket.

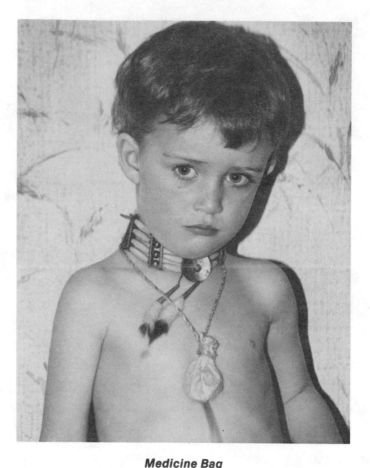

Medicine Bag
This bag is made from the scrotum of a mule deer, but any leather bag will do.

If a scrotum is not available, any soft leather can be used. The same pattern used for a "possible bag" can be used, only scaled down to the desired size.

What the medicine bag holds depends entirely on what the person who makes the bag wants. Hair, bone, animal parts, lighting wood, etc., are carried according to what physical traits the owner would like to acquire.

Possible Bag: The amount of leather needed to make a possible bag depends on the size of bag desired. Medium-soft two- to four-ounce leather works best.

A simple pattern to make is a rectangular piece of leather one inch wider and three times as long as the finished bag is to be.

The leather is folded, in thirds, lengthwise. The middle third and one end are sewn together along each outside edge with the leather wrong side out. The bottom corners can be rounded off to make a round bottom instead of a square bag. Turn the bag right side out after it is sewn. The remaining third is used as a flap and can be cut into long fringe two-thirds up the flap. The tip of a deer antler can be drilled and a leather thong fastened to it. The thong is tied to the bag and a buttonhole made in the flap for the antler tip to be passed through.

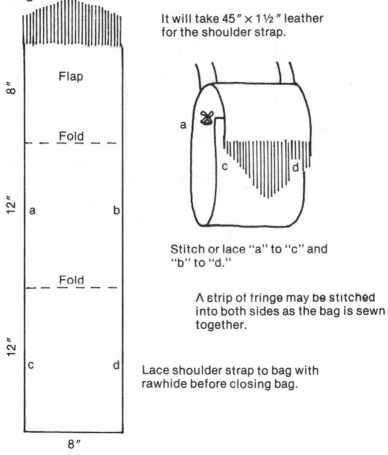

It will take 45″ × 1½″ leather for the shoulder strap.

Stitch or lace "a" to "c" and "b" to "d."

A strip of fringe may be stitched into both sides as the bag is sewn together.

Lace shoulder strap to bag with rawhide before closing bag.

Possible Bag

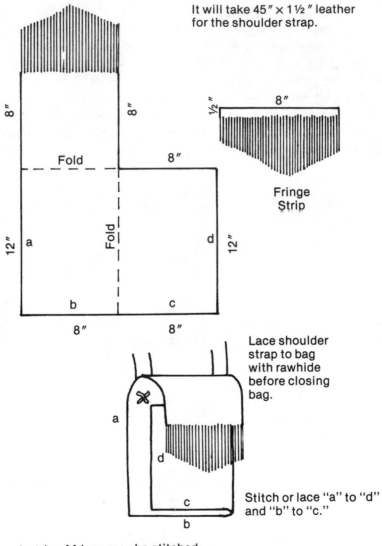

It will take 45″ × 1½″ leather for the shoulder strap.

8″

8″

Fold

8″

12″ a

Fold

d

12″

b

c

8″   8″

½″   8″

Fringe Strip

Lace shoulder strap to bag with rawhide before closing bag.

a

d

c

b

Stitch or lace "a" to "d" and "b" to "c."

A strip of fringe may be stitched into the bottom as the bag is sewn together.

Possible Bag

The possible bag can be decorated with beadwork and bells.

A possible bag is used to carry anything and everything when leather clothes without pockets are worn. The mountain men carried lead, patching, flint, etc., in his possible bag.

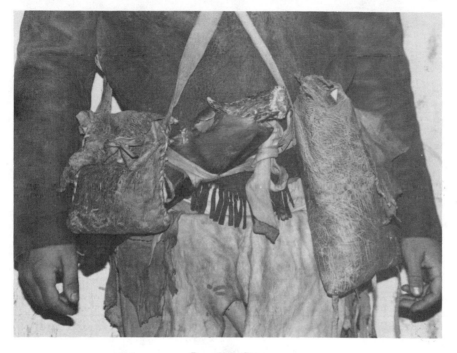

Possible Bags
The bag on the left is a bottom-fold pattern laced with rawhide. The bag on the right is a side-fold pattern sewed with heavy thread.

Packsack: A packsack requires one deer hide of medium-soft chrome tan. If a deer hide is unavailable, a medium-soft three- to four-ounce chrome-tan leather will do.

Following the pattern (page 100) the leather is cut and laced together with leather lacing bought commercially or cut as described in chapter 4, "Cutting Leather and Lacing." If it is sewn, a heavy waxed linen thread should be used.

Shoulder straps can be made from leather with ties or buckles for adjustment. Belts, webbing, or leather may be purchased at thrift stores and improvised. Commercial shoulder straps are available at mountaineering shops and can be adapted, with the addition of some buckles, to the pack.

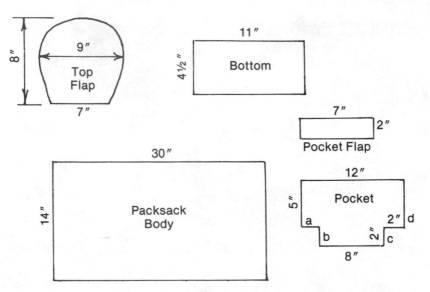

8" **9"** Top Flap **7"**

11" Bottom **4½"**

7" Pocket Flap **2"**

30" Packsack Body **14"**

12" Pocket **5"** a b 2" 2" c d **8"**

Sew or lace "a" to "b" and "c" to "d."

Shoulder straps should be 16" long and 2" wide. Use the same buckle system as on the toddler packsack.

Draw string at top to close packsack before closing the top flap.

Leather Packsack

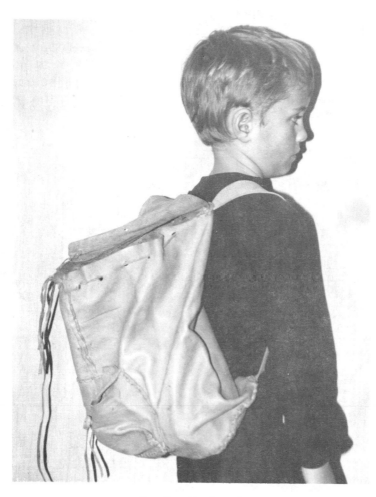

Leather Packsack

Ammunition Bag: An ammo bag is a drawstring bag that can have many uses besides carrying ammunition. It is made from a soft deerskin or similar leather and is easy to make. First, cut a rectangular piece of material one inch wider and twice as long as the finished bag. The leather is folded in half lengthwise and sewed up each side with the leather wrong side out. Turn the bag right side out after it is sewn. Using a punch, put holes along the bag opening one-half inch from the top. A soft leather lace a half inch wide is laced through the holes to draw the bag closed.

Dog Pack: Dog packs are made from medium heavy six- to eight-ounce soft oil-tan or Latigo-type leather, stitched with heavy waxed linen thread and riveted at all stress points.

Using the pattern as a guide, make a pattern to fit your size of dog using brown-paper grocery sacks or scrap-cloth material. Continue to check size adjustments on the dog as the pieces are stitched together.

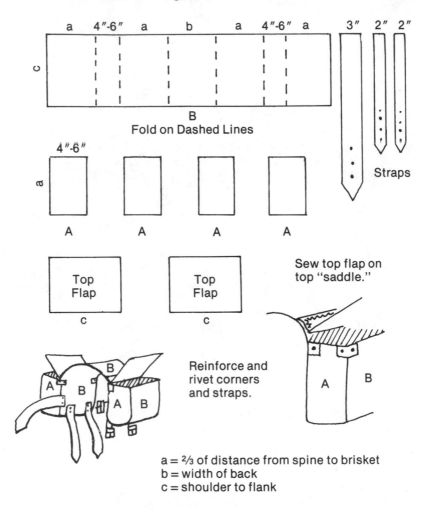

a = ⅔ of distance from spine to brisket
b = width of back
c = shoulder to flank

The dog pack must be measured to your dog, following the pattern.

Dog Pack

Purse: Purses may be made from either soft or hard, chrome- or vegetable-tanned leather depending on the desired product. The most commonly used leather is vegetable tan four-ounce stiff.

An easy purse may be made in the same style as the ammunition bag with a draw string and with the addition of a shoulder strap.

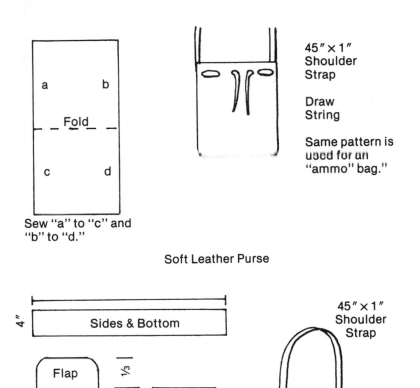

Sew "a" to "c" and "b" to "d."

45″ × 1″ Shoulder Strap

Draw String

Same pattern is used for an "ammo" bag.

Soft Leather Purse

Sides & Bottom
4″

Flap
Back
1/3
2/3
a   Front   a
a

45″ × 1″ Shoulder Strap

Heighth and Width as Desired

L = a + a + a

Hard Leather Purse

Purse

The pattern shown requires four-ounce vegetable-tan leather although the amount will vary according to the size of purse wanted. Draw your pattern size on paper and calculate the square footage you will need. The pieces should be laced together—or sewn with waxed thread—each giving a different effect.

A clasp can be purchased or a single strap placed across the purse, as illustrated, to tuck the flap under.

Money Clip: A two-ounce eight-by-three-inch piece of vegetable tan, medium-soft leather is needed to make a money clip. A medium size snap and a metal money "clip" is also required. Dampen the leather and fold as shown in the illustration. Punch a hole for the snap and secure the snap in place. The clip is attached by sliding it on the appropriate fold then the money clip is finished.

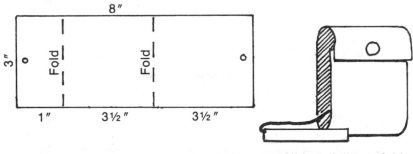

Slide "clip" onto fold.

Money Clip

Wallet: Wallets are normally made from a vegetable-tan leather in the two- to three-ounce range. Depending on the desired finished product, other types of leather may be used. Draw a pattern on paper to the full size of the wallet desired and determine the amount of leather needed. Lacing is required. Measure the area to be laced and go one and a half times longer to determine the length of the lacing needed.

If vegetable-tan leather is used it may be dampened to make the fold lay more smoothly.

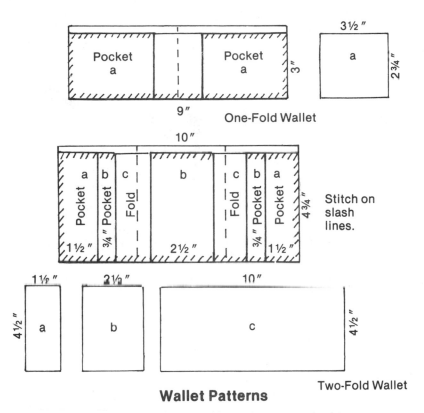

Wallet Patterns

Sheaths

Open Blade: Knife sheaths are made from vegetable-tan leather, Latigo, or rawhide. An attractive sheath can be made from the foreleg of a moose or an elk without tanning. The fresh hide is scraped of all flesh and fat, then stretched over a form generally made from wood and laced in place with wet rawhide lacing. (When using rawhide lacing put a pin or needle through the lacing after tying the knot to prevent the shrinking strip from untying the knot.) This method works well for mountain-man styles.

Using the patterns as guides make a pattern on paper for the size of your knife—leather or rawhide work well—then lace with rawhide since the blade will not cut the rawhide lacing, but the blade will cut leather lacing and rivets will dull the knife blade.

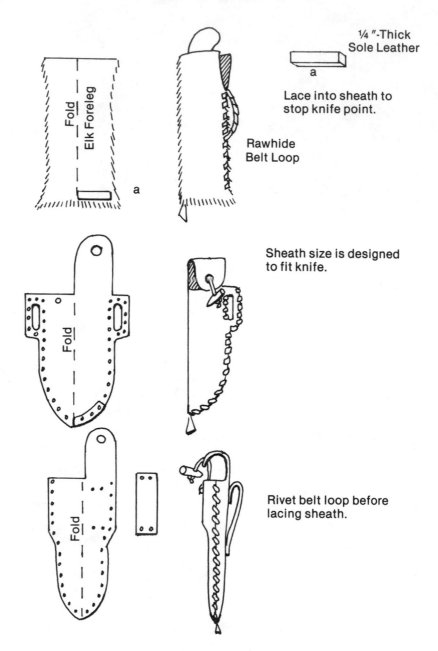

Fold

Elk Foreleg

a

¼ "-Thick
Sole Leather

a

Lace into sheath to
stop knife point.

Rawhide
Belt Loop

Sheath size is designed
to fit knife.

Fold

Fold

Rivet belt loop before
lacing sheath.

Open-Blade Knife Sheaths

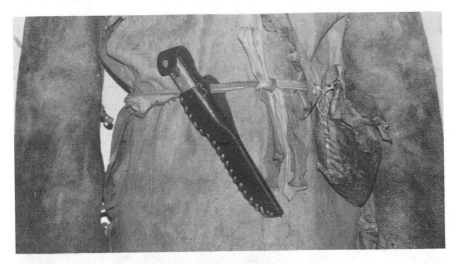

Formed Open-Blade Knife Sheath

By wetting the leather the sheath is formed to the shape of the knife then laced with rawhide. The knife is held in place by a flap held down with a toggle fastener. The fastener has been removed to show the location of holes where the fastener would be attached.

Open-Blade Knife Sheath with Toggle Fastener

The sheath is one-piece construction, laced with rawhide. The belt loop is cut as a part of the pattern. The knife is held in place by a flap held down with the deer-antler toggle-fastener.

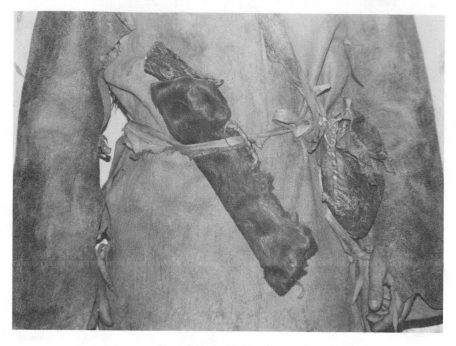

Open-Blade Knife Sheath
This sheath is one-piece construction from the foreleg of an elk. It is laced with rawhide and the rawhide wrap is used for a belt loop.

Closed Blade: Knife sheaths for closing blades are made from vegetable-tan leather, Latigo, or rawhide. Leather lacing, rawhide lacing, waxed linen thread, or rivets may be used for making the sheath.

Using the patterns as guides, draw a pattern on paper to fit your knife. If you are using vegetable tan or Latigo the leather can be waxed after the product is finished. Rawhide must be soaked then the excess water removed. It is then stretched on a form to be stitched together, preferably with rawhide lacing. Vegetable-tan leather can be dampened and shaped on a form as discussed in chapter 4.

Pliers/Screwdriver: These covers are generally made from Latigo and laced with leather lacing, or they are riveted.

Using the pattern as a reference, draw a pattern on paper to fit your pliers and screwdriver. To help it wear better the leather can be waxed after the product is finished.

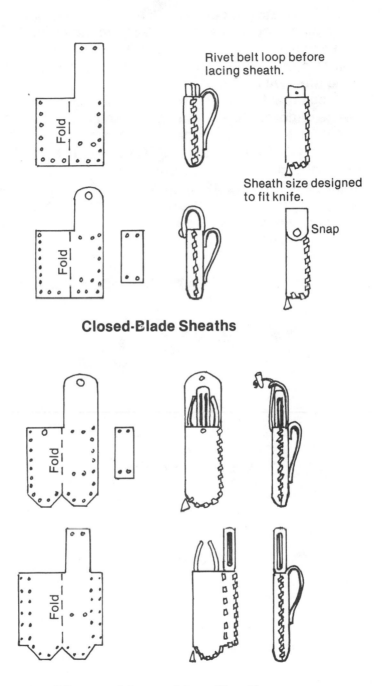

Rivet belt loop before lacing sheath.

Sheath size designed to fit knife.

Snap

Closed-Blade Sheaths

Pliers and Screwdriver Sheaths

Rifle: Scabbard or sheaths can be made from almost any type of oil- or vegetable-tan leather depending on the desired effect and the use. A simple cover for protection or for mountain-man attire is made from soft suede, buckskin, or any soft two- to four-ounce oil-tan leather.

A scabbard to be used with a horse—or where the rifle must be removed from it with speed and one hand—should be made with a stiff four- to six-ounce vegetable-tan leather or rawhide that is lined with a soft leather. If rawhide is to be used, it should be domestic cow with the hair attached which will place hair on the outside. Adjust the desired pattern to your gun and draw the scabbard on paper to calculate the amount of leather or rawhide needed.

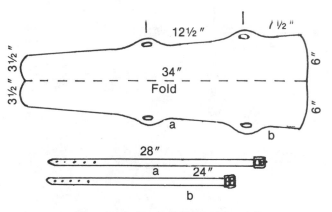

Standard-size saddle scabbard. It may need to be adjusted to your gun.

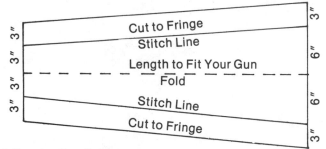

Black Powder Gun Cover

Rifle Sheath

The vegetable-tan leather should be dampened before shaping and before lacing, stitching, or riveting. The rawhide is stretched over a frame and tacked down to dry. It cannot be laced until the soft leather liner is glued and stitched in place and that cannot be done until the rawhide is shaped and dried. Then the pieces are laced together with wet rawhide.

Pistol: Scabbards or sheaths for handguns should be made from a stiff vegetable-tan leather although any stiff leather will work if it is lined with oil or vegetable-tan leather. The gun should not have continual contact with chrome-tan leather because the chemicals will cause a blued pistol or rifle to rust.

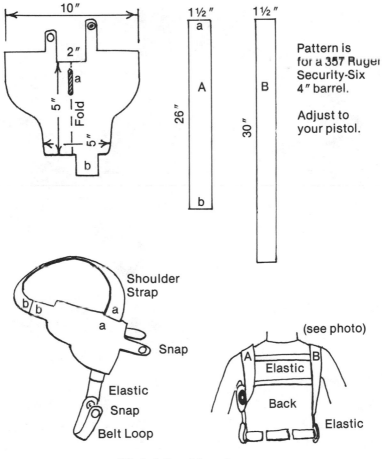

Pistol Scabbard

Shoulder Holster

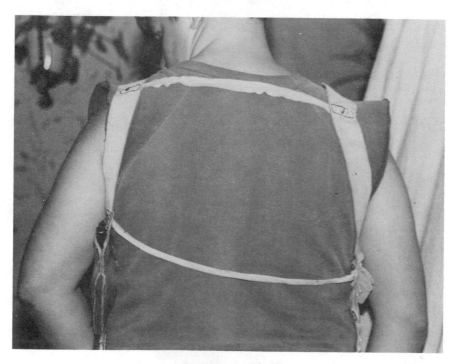

Shoulder Holster

Adjust the patterns to your pistol. Draw it on paper and calculate the amount of leather needed. The pieces can be stitched, laced, riveted, or use a combination of any of the three.

Covers

Book: Bookcovers are made from fine, soft suede or buckskin two-ounce leather. They are generally laced with commercial lacing of contrasting color.

Follow the pattern and place the book on paper to create a pattern to fit your book. Determine the amount of leather and lacing needed.

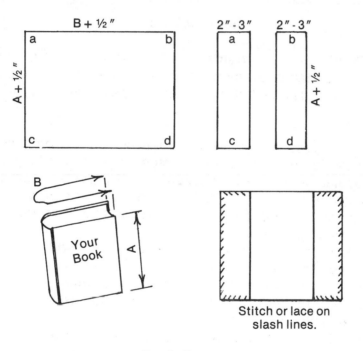

Stitch or lace on
slash lines.

Book Cover

Checkbook: Checkbook covers should be made from medium-soft two-ounce leather. An attractive cover can be made from unborn calf or from any short-hair skin. Lacing is needed.

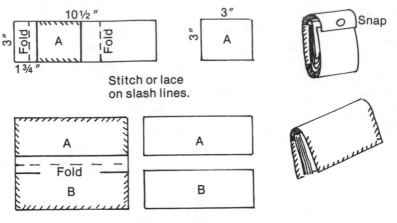

Checkbook Covers

Credit Card: A carrying case for credit cards requires any medium-soft tan two-ounce leather with or without hair. Lacing will be needed and plastic windows may also be used.

Rawhide

Carry Case: Special cases can be made from rawhide and made for many different articles. Rawhide works well for a binocular case because the hard cover provides protection. Leaving the hair on, and putting it on the outside when the case is constructed, gives additional padding to articles such as binoculars, cameras, etc.

A simple construction is a box with a flap and a belt loop, if desired. The belt loop is fastened on before the case is made. The case is made from one rectangular piece of wet rawhide stretched over a form the size of the article and laced with wet rawhide lacing.

The flap must be pounded with a rounded hammer (ball peen) on a medium-soft surface to soften it so that it will bend to open and shut. The flap should be tacked closed while it dries so that it will stay shut.

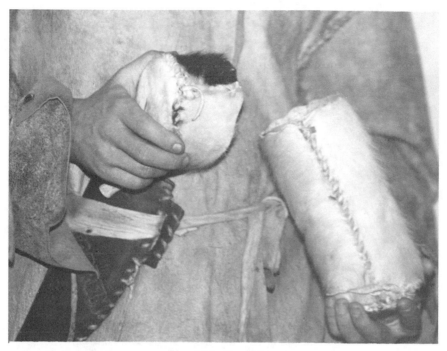

Rawhide Container
This container has the hair left on and is laced with rawhide.

Parfleche (an early Indian suitcase): Parfleches were used for storing dried food, meat, and roots and for carrying clothes. Everything the Indians had they carried and stored in the parfleche.

Commercial rawhide is too thick and too stiff to be used for a parfleche. Originals were made from buffalo rawhide, but since buffalo rawhide is not easy to come by nowadays a young cow, deer, or elk will do. (Elk is preferred.) The skin is processed into rawhide as discussed in chapter 3. The rawhide is pounded with a rounded hammer along the bend lines (see illustration). Holes are burned or punched into the flap ends and leather lacing tied into them. A glaze, as discussed in chapter 3, can be placed on the outside to help waterproof the storage case. A parfleche can be made any size needed.

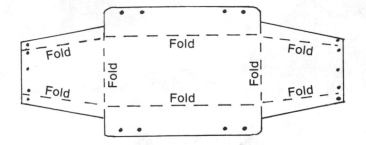

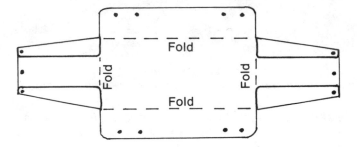

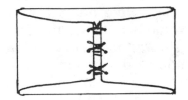

Parfleche

Windows: Old-fashioned windows are made from deer-skin rawhide. The hide is soaked to remove the hair, as discussed in chapter 3. The hair is removed and the skin is stretched over the window opening as tightly as possible while the skin is wet. It must be fastened securely because tremendous pressure will be exerted on the fasteners when the rawhide dries. After it is dry, a mixture of tallow and beeswax is melted and rubbed over the outside to help waterproof the rawhide.

You can't see through a rawhide window but it does let light in.

Drums: Drums are made by stretching dehaired, wet rawhide over a willow hoop or hollow tube, can, log, barrel, etc. The skins can be stretched over both ends and laced together with wet rawhide lacing or only placed on one end of the drum and tacked down to dry.

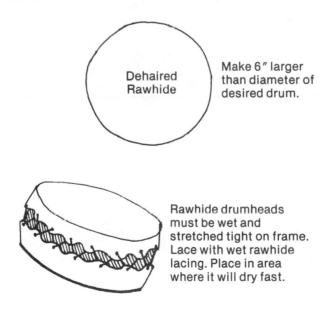

Dehaired
Rawhide

Make 6″ larger
than diameter of
desired drum.

Rawhide drumheads
must be wet and
stretched tight on frame.
Lace with wet rawhide
lacing. Place in area
where it will dry fast.

Drum

War Shield: War shields are made from heavy rawhide. The Indians made them from the top of the buffalo's hump. The neck and shoulders of bull elk, or domestic bull, provide a thick, tough hide for a shield.

The green hide is soaked, as discussed in chapter 3, to remove the hair. The holes to attach handles should be punched in the right places. The holes should be small since they will become larger as the skin dries. The wet rawhide is then laid out and staked in the desired shape. The skin should not be stretched—just laid out tight. Stretching will make a thinner shield.

The rawhide for a shield should be shrunk to make it thicker.

One method is to stake over a pit of hot rocks and move the stakes in as the hide shrinks.

The hide should be cut twice as large as the shield desired. The shield is slightly wider than your chest. Another method of shrinking is to repeatedly wet and stake to shrink in the sun.

Shoulder Strap for Field Carry

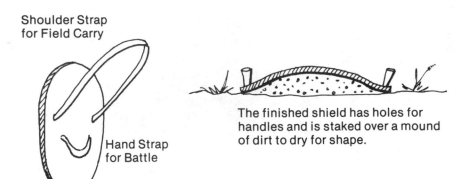

Hand Strap for Battle

The finished shield has holes for handles and is staked over a mound of dirt to dry for shape.

War Shield

When the hide is dry, stiff, and hard, wet rawhide handles are attached with wet rawhide lacing. The handles are placed over forms, and allowed to dry to the desired size and shape.

Furniture

Three-legged Camp Stool: One square foot of three- to four-ounce Latigo or vegetable-tan leather is needed for each stool. The leather can be laced, stitched, or riveted. The stool also requires three three-quarter-inch by one-inch hardwood of the same length.

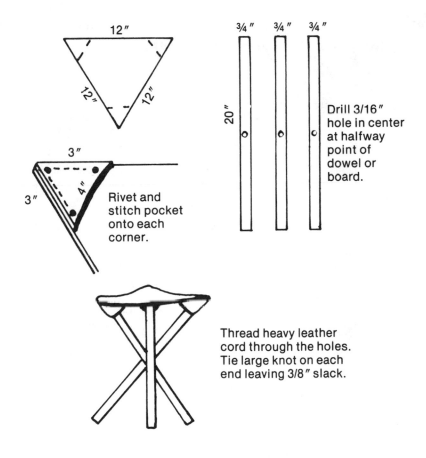

Rivet and stitch pocket onto each corner.

Drill 3/16" hole in center at halfway point of dowel or board.

Thread heavy leather cord through the holes. Tie large knot on each end leaving 3/8" slack.

Three-Legged Camp Stool

Four-Legged Camp Stool: This stool uses a sixteen-inch by 12-inch piece of three- to four-ounce Latigo or vegetable-tan leather. Other materials needed are:
- Brass tacks
    - Four pieces of one-inch by one-inch by twenty-inch hardwood
    - Two pieces of one-inch by one-inch by fourteen-inch hardwood
    - Two one-half-inch by thirteen-inch hardwood dowels
    - Two number eight by two-inch machine bolts
    - Four washers
    - Two nuts
    - Eight one-inch wood screws

The wood frame is made like the illustration and the leather is tacked to the cross members.

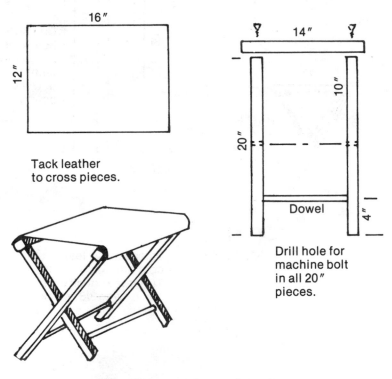

Four-Legged Camp Stool

Plant Hanger: These decorations are generally made from scrap leather. The leather must be soft, two-ounce, and generally oil or chrome tan. The pot-holding section is cut as shown in the illustration to allow it to expand. The original size of the leather before cutting depends on the size of flower-pot to be hung. Four one-inch-wide leather straps are cut to be attached to the potholder using a slit as illustrated. The straps are tied together at the top to hang on a hook.

Miscellaneous

Rawhide Hammer: A rawhide hammer is made from heavy domestic-bull rawhide. A strip one-half inch wider than the finished hammerhead and about a twelve-inch-long strip of rawhide is needed. Nails and a hammer handle are also required. The rawhide is soaked and rolled as illustrated. The outer edge is nailed into the roll and the product set to dry. It is helpful to wrap the roll with material or tape on the outer ends while it dries. After it is dry, drill a hole for the handle (generally must be made oblong, not round) and the hammer is finished.

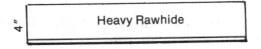

Length determined by desired diameter of hammerhead.

Rawhide Hammer

Leather Hinges: Hinges are easily made with heavy six-ounce Latigo or vegetable-tan leather. While leather hinges will not support a door as well as metal hinges will, they still do a satisfactory job. If vegetable-tan is used it should be oiled and waxed to help withstand the weather. The longer the hinges are, vertically, the better support they will give. They are nailed or placed with wood screws to the door and frame.

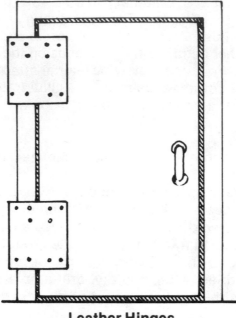

Leather Hinges

Leather Doll: Dolls are made and used the way a paper doll set is used but with leather instead of paper. The doll is cut from scraps of stiff four-ounce vegetable-tan leather. The clothes are made from scraps of suede or other soft leather odds and ends. The clothes can be attached with Velcro or with string ties. Your imagination is the only limit to what can be done with these dolls.

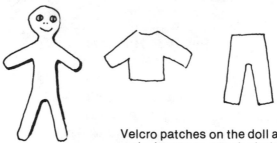

Velcro patches on the doll and clothing make it easy to attach clothing.

Leather Dolls

Knife Handle: A knife handle is made from heavy six-ounce vegetable-tan leather. The leather is cut into discs which will be the diameter desired for the handle. A slot or hole—whichever will fit the knife tang—is cut in the center of the discs. The discs are then slipped onto the knife tang and contact glue put between each disc. After all the discs are on, a nut can be screwed on the top of the tang to hold the discs on if the tang is threaded. Some tangs will pound out flat like a rivet on the end over a flat washer. A method of finishing off the end of the tang must be devised to hold the disc on, depending on the tang.

When the top of the tang is finished off, and the glue is dry, the discs are sanded and shaped to the desired handle shape.

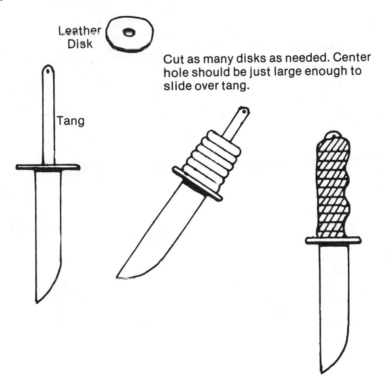

Leather Disk

Cut as many disks as needed. Center hole should be just large enough to slide over tang.

Tang

Leather Knife Handle

Supply Sources

Look in the yellow pages of the phone book under *Leather, Tanners,* and *Taxidermist.* This will either give you an outlet for supplies or give you contact with someone who will know where you can find what you need. Following is a list of suppliers:

Tanning Supplies

American Tanners Association
411 Fifth Avenue
New York, New York 10016

J. W. Elwood Supply Co., Inc.
1202 Harney, Box 3507
Omaha, Nebraska 68103

Leather Supplies

Check local phone listing, or write:

Tandy Leather Company
P.O. Box 791
Fort Worth, Texas 76101
Free catalog

Amber Leather Co.
835 San Julian
Los Angeles, California 90052
Scrap leather by the pound

Roberta Creative Leathers
296 Donlea
Barrington, Illinois 60010
Knitting and macrame thongs; precut designs

Beggs & Cobb, Inc.
171 Madison Avenue
New York, New York 10016
Reptile

Tools

Tandy Leather Company
Check local phone listing

Ace Hardware Stores
Check local phone listing

MacPherson Leather Co.
200 South Los Angeles Street
Los Angeles, California 90052

C. S. Osborne
Harrison, New Jersey 07029
Catalog, price list, local distributors

Cements and Glues

Darge Cement
100 Jacksonville Road
Towaco, New Jersey 07082

Tandy Leather Company
Check local phone listing
Craftsman all-purpose cement

U.S. Plywood Co.
2305 Superior Street
Kalamazoo, Michigan 49003

Dyes

Tandy Leather Company
Check local phone listing

Fezandie & Bros., Inc.
103 Lafayette Street
New York, New York 10013
Leather and batik dyes

Index